T0158784

{Nobody's Favorite

Nobody's Favorite

A Memoir By
Victoria Stott

iUniverse

NOBODY'S FAVORITE
A MEMOIR

iUniverse books may be ordered through booksellers or by contacting:

iUniverse
1663 Liberty Drive
Bloomington, IN 47403
www.iuniverse.com
1-800-Authors (1-800-288-4677)

ISBN: 978-1-5320-0735-4 (sc)
ISBN: 978-1-5320-0736-1 (e)

Library of Congress Control Number: 2016917596

Print information available on the last page.

iUniverse rev. date: 10/26/2016

{ THIS STORY IS DEDICATED...

To all those who have suffered abuse in any of its forms; may you achieve victory over its effects.

To my children; "I love you."

To all those in uniform bearing arms in the service of securing our safety, freedom and human rights and to their families; of whose service and sacrifice we are all indebted.

To the myriad of heroes who work with youth; coaches, teachers, mentors, counsellors, leaders and champions. The value of your contribution to the character of others is infinite.

ACKNOWLEDGEMENTS

I acknowledge first my God and King, my Lord and Savior; Yeshua HaMashiac, Jesus Christ the Messiah and His Holy Spirit, from whom comes all life.

The many people whose lives have crossed paths with mine and especially those who helped changed the trajectory of my life. I wish I could write your names here but cannot; you have helped me save my life. Thank you.

CONTENTS

Chapter 1   Living Oblivious 1

Chapter 2   Forming Insignificance 11

Chapter 3   Fortifying Insignificance 31

Chapter 4   Creating Invisibility 61

Chapter 5   Smashing into Stillness 69

Chapter 6   Finding the Beginning 81

Chapter 7   Colliding with Life 91

Chapter 8   Speaking the Truth 97

Chapter 9   Hunting for Worms 103

Chapter 10 Destroying Deception 119

Chapter 11 Experiencing Living 135

INTRODUCTION

Childhood trauma and neglect shattered my ability to feel safe at too young an age and defined my identity, the meaning of my life, the story of my life and my self concept until I was able to challenge myself and see me differently.

Denial and deception played a much bigger part in my story than I could ever have imagined as these were a necessary inclusion in the daily life of the family I grew up in. Secrets and lies in the family preceded my arrival from the orphanage.

I am no different than any human being keeping secrets. Everybody keeps secrets of some sort during their lifetime. In the beginning I kept secrets under the threat of death and to avoid harm. In the end shame kept my secrets hidden-even from me in some instances. I came to learn that the secrets kept by other members of my family and my father in particular were predestined to create an ideal environment in which I was plagued by invisibility and insignificance.

The writing of this memoir was my way of declaring war on the effects of trauma in my life. My primary goal was to expose the shameful secrets I have kept hidden and validate myself. I decided to face each of the areas of stunted development in my mind and see what could be done to foster growth in them. Writing was the easier part. Sharing my story with you is more difficult.

In sharing my story, I hope to encourage others to protect and pursue wellness for themselves. With few resources and little support, I have been able to achieve outcomes beyond my expectations. Despite the exertion required to heal; my journey has been worth the effort. I have peace.

Yet, change is needed. Our policing and justice systems must recognise their place in trauma survivor's lives. Social Services, education and mental heath services must utilize a trauma focused approach in planning the delivery of services to survivors. I have shared my experiences with each of these in my memoir. The cracks in our systems existed thirty years ago. They exist today. Use my story to add a victim's voice to your discussion.

With quiet assurance I hope that my story inspires you. I hope that within the narrative, you find something that makes you laugh. I try to laugh as much as I can. I hope you find beauty. I have found breathtaking beauty in my life despite the ugliness that dwelt alongside it. If I can challenge your thinking as I did my own perhaps something good will come of it. And I hope that something you read will motivate you to choose life. In whatever form life is for you; because its power is infinite and it triumphs over all.

As I write this, The Tragically Hip have just performed their last concert. Canada has done well in the Olympics. The universe continues to unfold as it should.

This is for us.

Victoria

CHAPTER ONE

Living Oblivious

"The most effective way to destroy people is to deny and obliterate their own understanding of their history".

George Orwell

On Wednesday September 2, 1998, Swiss Air Flight 111 plunged into the Atlantic Ocean off the coast of Peggy's Cove killing all 229 people aboard. This was the second highest death toll of any air disaster in the history of Canada after Arrow Air Flight 1285.

I had the opportunity shortly after this event to accept an invitation to attend church. I had been invited to attend this church several times but I was not interested in church. More to the point I was not interested in God.

I had had enough of God. Brought up in the Roman Catholic Church, ours was a faithful family. I was a good catholic girl and we were good catholic people. I was an army brat and we lived on several armed forces base's during my childhood until my father retired and moved us to a small town in a small province. While on the base's my father served the church by teaching catechism, taking care of the weekly offering and training and mentoring the altar servers. My Mother did the laundry of the base priest and it was often we had a clergy to the house for supper. We believed in God, did our good works and were faithful in giving.

I felt confident in being part of the largest church on earth. I was taught that Roman Catholicism was the only true religion, all other religions were false. Protestants were "protesters", they protested against the laws of God. I was taught that since Protestants were not obedient to God they were not destined for heaven. I was discouraged from befriending anyone who was a protestant.

Someone gave me a new testament in grade three and I read it. I underlined certain verses that made sense to me at the time but I had questions. When I asked questions I was often told to be a good girl and not ask questions. If the question was simple enough I was sometimes given an answer or explanation. I can't remember the questions I asked but on more than one occasion I was told that we mere humans cannot understand God or the Bible and I should not read it and just accept by faith the things I could understand. I was told to obey my parents and leave the rest alone.

By the fall of 1998, I was convinced that God was a punisher and that he had decided to punish me from an early age. I had never understood why I deserved such a fate except for the day on the swing when I was three years old declaring my hatred for Him. I knew that since I had sinned so much I was destined for hell, there was no hope for me from a God who judged me unworthy and whose laws and commandments I was unable to keep.

Born in Montreal, Quebec in late 1967; a secret bastard daughter was brought home to a family consisting of a woman living a double life hiding her shame of unmarried motherhood, a sister eight years old, and a brother, a year younger. I must have come to know my family in my infant, preverbal state but I have no conscious memory of the loss of them. Three children were apprehended by child protection services and sent to an orphanage. I have no memory of this orphanage or of being snatched from my family. As the youngest, a baby around eighteen months old I was kept separate from my siblings and any sense of family that I had known.

I was adopted in 1969. I know little about my orphanage experience; only what was told to me many years later by people who had been there. A friend visited once thinking she may leave a child there. She decided against it because she could not leave her child in such a place She described the orphanage as a very dark place that had little love in it.

I met my siblings at the age of thirty They remember the orphanage and their experiences there. My sister describes the orphanage as the best home she'd ever had.

I have no memory of my first home in this new adopted family. No memory of the home on an ordinary street in an ordinary Canadian small town. I can point out the house we lived in while driving past it to this day; not knowing exactly the atmosphere held within it when I was brought there.

My new family. Mother from a small Acadian fishing village, a hard worker, father of Scottish descent, a member of the Canadian Armed Forces. A boy adopted four years earlier. An entry in a home visit report from a community services social worker several months later records the boy as being hostile and jealous towards me, a condition which permeated my early life and plagued our family for decades after.

The first home I do consciously remember was an apartment known as PMQ's or private military quarters. A red brick building on a Canadian Forces base. With a swing set off to the left, a sloping paved drive and a clothesline platform in the back. Grass lived on the other side from which the door led to a small field of sorts where we lit sparklers on Canada day.

Must have been 1971. It was this apartment we lived in when I found a stray kitten and brought it home. The kitten seemed hungry so I fed it a wiener from the fridge in the tiny galley style kitchen. I asked Daddy if I could keep it and he said yes. I was very happy. The next day, catching me in the middle of feeding the kitten another wiener; he became very angry and shouted. He banished the cat and made me eat the other half of the wiener. I thought it was gross. It had cat germs on it but I had to eat it because he said so.

Many years later he related to me why he banished the cat and was so angry with me. Apparently my father spent that first night cleaning up messes all over the apartment left by the first wiener. I wish he had explained it to me earlier because at the time I didn't understand what I had done wrong and why I was so bad.

We moved into another PMQ on the base just prior to my starting school at age four in 1971. I did like the house, it seemed large to me and the staircase had a curve. I remember Christmas there that first year. The tree stood tall in the curve of the staircase casting its glow of multi colored lights into the living room. I received a new Barbie doll that Christmas and a new flannel nightgown. In the summer I got my first bike and remember dad teaching me to ride it, holding the back of the seat to stabilize me. I was like any other little girl, curious, affectionate and cute. I had curly blonde hair that hung in ringlets around the sides of my face and lively blue eyes. That is until my mother had my hair cut short, like a boy's. It was too much trouble for my mother I think, keeping my hair in good order. My report cards from early school indicate that I was bright. Often my teachers commented that I was an inquisitive child and a constant chatterbox.

The military bases that I grew up on had excellent recreational programs and I learned to swim at an early age. I learned to tap dance, bowl and do gymnastics. I participated in a variety of sports but swimming was always my favorite. I wanted to be a lifeguard when I grew up. I was enrolled in brownies at age seven and I worked diligently at obtaining my badges. The badge for sewing gave me the most trouble but the others came easily to me.

I liked to play with dolls, Barbie's in particular. My mother had an old white metal stand with three shelves that I used for a Barbie house. I would make dresses for my Barbie's from the bits of fabric that had to be cut from the bottom of my pants. My pants were always too long and needed hemming. The extra fabric was perfect for Barbie dresses. On Saturday mornings I would get a bowl with some water and soap and wash the Barbie clothes and hang them to dry. I used the little plastic trays that the tomatoes came in for Barbie beds in my doll house. I named my favorite Barbie doll Love.

I loved animals; dogs, cats and horses especially. On Sunday afternoon after church and dinner I would watch Mutual of Omaha on TV. I was awed at the images of animals in the wild. I thought lions were majestic and elephants were magnificent.

I had a special fondness for nature and I loved to walk through wooded areas. I liked to climb trees. I would explore my surroundings and I loved to get across any body of water that I found. I was always excited to find tadpoles. I would go back to the same spot to see them every day waiting for the day when they would turn into frogs. If there was a frog I would try to catch it. I would hold it and study it for a while before letting it go. I was careful not to hurt the frogs and the other kids said I was the best at catching them.

The second base we lived on was near an Indian reservation. One day I crossed the creek that was between me and the perimeter fence. It was hard getting across the creek. The water underneath was deep and fast moving but there was a fallen tree trunk over the creek and I balanced myself as I shimmied across.

I wanted to see some Indians. There was much talk from the kids on the base about the Indians, how they were bad and we were good. A common game was cowboys and Indians. Whomever the leader was that day declared which side you were on. It was best to be on the cowboy side so you would not endure the punishment of being captured and scalped. The kids said scalping would happen for real if one of us were captured by them.

When I got to the chain link fence there was a little Indian girl on the other side. I tried to talk to her and she tried to talk to me. She did not speak English and I did not speak her language so we just looked at each other for a while, smiling at each other. I came back the next day to see if she would be there and she was. We started meeting at the same spot each day after school. We were never able to talk to each other we communicated. I brought her a picture I had drawn of her and me. I rolled up the picture and pushed it through one of the links in the fence and the next day she had a picture she had drawn for me.

I called her Karen because I didn't know her name. She remained my special secret friend until the day I fell into the creek. I came home wet, crying and bleeding. When my mother found out where I had been she forbade me to go to the perimeter fence again. *You could have drowned. Look at the mess you made of yourself; look at the mess you've made of this house!.* I was very sad not to see my friend anymore. For Christmas I received a little Indian girl doll. I named her Karen. She was my favorite doll for a long time after that.

My teacher that year was an Indian too. I was in grade two and I thought my teacher was beautiful. She had the longest hair that I had ever seen. Her hair was shiny black and straight. It hung down her back and almost reached her bum. She played guitar and she would sing us Indian songs on Friday afternoons. She was so nice. I thought she was the princess Pocahontas.

The winter was fun on this base. There was an ice festival where teams would make fantastic giant ice sculptures. They painted them. I saw a giant hamburger, giant castles, and replicas of military vehicles or buildings. All kinds of animals were made and I was in awe of what could be done with the vast amounts of snow. They would water the sculptures to make them freeze. There were real igloos. You could go inside. You had to crawl through the doorway to get in but once inside they seemed large. They had a small hole in the very top for the smoke to rise out. The family would have a fire in the middle of the igloo. The family members would sit around the fire warming themselves, melting snow for water. Cooking whatever animal the father killed. I could hardly imagine a family would actually live like that. I got to see an igloo being built from nothing but a pile of snow. It was cool to watch. Rectangle shaped bricks were placed in an exact sequence. It was mudded with snow and frozen with water. It was awesome.

One weekend my father told me the pool would be closed to the kids on the base. The base would allow kids from the reservation to swim on Friday night. The pool would be drained and scrubbed before being re-filled for us. I was desperate to see my friend Karen and wondered if she would be among the kids swimming. I begged my father to allow me to swim with them. He permitted it. I got to swim but Karen was not there. It was still fun because without using words I was able to show some kids some tricks I knew. Back flips, cannon balls diving head first into the deep end. In the shallow end I taught the kids handstands and somersaults and how to pick things up from the bottom. I helped a couple of them float on top, not letting them sink. A few were afraid but I tried to show them that they didn't need to be, water is fun.

I developed a boil on my left shin in the days following. It was a gross mass of puss and yuk and it hurt a lot. My mother said, *"that's what you get from swimming with dirty Indians"*. She wouldn't help me with it. She thought it was disgusting. I was- for wanting to swim with them. My Nana came from Ottawa. My mother lied to my Nana; she said I would not allow her to touch it. I can't remember how long nana stayed, she taught me how to take care of the boil and I still have the scar on my leg to remember that she came to help me.

We stayed one year on this base. My father helped close it. In grade three we moved to another base. If I had to choose a favorite base this would be the one. I watched my first Canadian Olympic games while on this base. I met the queen. I listened to Elvis Presley and cried the day he died.

We lived on a crescent. Across the street behind the houses was a wooded area. Footpaths ran through it with plenty of large beautiful trees. To me it was a forest. Beside the forest was a playground and a large field. The playground had my favorites, swings and monkey bars. There was a sand pit, perfect for playing dinky cars with the boys.

I loved the forest and wandered through it daily and climbed the trees. If I found an animal that was hurt, I would bring it home and put it into a box. I would feed it bread soaked in water or milk. Several birds with broken wings were nursed to health in this way. Once when the bird I was nursing died in the night I was heartbroken. I brought the bird to the base priest. He helped me to pray for the bird. We buried it in a box in the chapel yard. I made a little cross out of Popsicle sticks to mark the spot.

Some people came to my classroom. They were putting on a play for Christmas and they needed a little girl to cast for a role. All the girls in class were lined up against the back wall and given a line to say out loud. They told us they needed someone with a loud voice. We were instructed to say the line as loud as we could. I got the part in the play because my voice was the loudest. Some of the other girls were mad at me because of that but I ignored them when they said I wouldn't be any good in the play. I think I was good.

As I grew I got better and better at climbing trees, hoping creeks and catching animals. The monkey bars were fun for me and I was the only one brave enough to try walking across the top. I learned to skip stones and I tried my best to beat the boys when they challenged a stone skip, a frog catch or a tree climb. I played less and less with Barbie's and dolls.

CHAPTER TWO

Forming Insignificance

My first memory of acknowledging
God is from when I was three
years old. I was sitting on a swing,
swinging back and forth as high
as I could, screaming at the top
of my lungs, "I hate you God, I
hate you!!"

Victoria Stott

My brother hated me. I was better than him at almost everything. I was smarter in school and I always made friends. He didn't have any. He had always hated me.

I hate you and I'm going to kill you. When I was three years old he tried to carry out his threat. The brick apartment building had the wooden landing structure for clotheslines. I was sitting, back to the edge of the clothesline landing playing with a Barbie doll one day when he said it, "I hate you and I'm going to kill you". In one swift motion, he pushed me off the landing. I fell backwards six feet onto the pavement. This incident fractured my skull. My mother came and picked me up. *He pushed me, I need a doctor* . A man offered to drive us to the hospital. My mother told him I fell when he asked what happened. I saw my brothers tiny wicked grin when he heard that. My father was away when it happened. My father was often away.

On another day, I was sitting in a wagon at the top of the pavement near the doors. *I'm going to kill you* and pushed the wagon down the slope directly into the path of an oncoming car. I was really scared of running into the car. Luckily the driver saw what happened and was able to avoid a collision. It was me the driver yelled at for being so careless. Then, the small wicked smile; satisfaction on my brother's face. I held my fear and my tears deep inside, trying hard for him not to see.

Once my brother told me he was going to make me go blind. We were standing opposite each other on either side of the coffee table in the living room. He had the can of furniture polish behind his back but I did not see it at first. He quickly pulled out the furniture polish from behind his back and sprayed as hard as he could directly into my eyes. I saw the look of hatred. I felt the sting and burning. I told my mother, she said

13

nothing to him but scolded me. I was told to rinse my eyes with water. Coming out of the bathroom, I was confronted by the small wicked grin on the face I was starting to hate.

When I think about my statements to God on the swing, I wonder what concept a three-year-old has of God. It is no mystery to me that I would have acquired an understanding of the concept of hate. I knew the look of hate on my brother's face and I knew that I was hated. I was hated by both my mother and brother. I knew that hatred was angry, violent and mean. But I wonder what I knew of God and how I knew whatever it was. I held him responsible for my being where I was, in a family that did not want me.

By the time I was in grade three, I knew my brother was a problem, not just to me but to everyone. He would often have angry outbursts. He was one of those kids that family remarked about; something is wrong with that boy. I made this comment to my father after one angry outburst, *he's a problem. He'll grow out of it.* That was the end of the conversation. We didn't have lengthy discussions in our house. Conversations between my parents and I were a few short sentences or directions. That was all. We did not spend time together as a family. I was rarely permitted to be in the room when adults were present. "He'll grow out of it" my father said. My brother never did.

His assaults against me became more frequent and more violent. Daily I was slapped, kicked, punched or pushed. Always the same comment, *I hate you* now adding, *you fucking bitch. I'm gunna get you. Just wait. You're dead.*

I would often come home to find things in my room destroyed. Toys would be broken, my barbie heads ripped off, clothes flung all over the room, my bed torn apart. I hated when he was in my room. Keeping my room and the entire house in perfect order was an absolute directive from my mother. We could be "inspected" at any time and if found derelict we could be kicked out and have nowhere to live. These were always temporary living quarters, never our home. They belonged to the Department of National Defence.

If I was in the room when he came in I would hide in the closet while he destroyed my things. I had already learned that it was no use telling on him. *He's just trying to get a reaction from you* my mother would say. *Just ignore him.* Nobody ever helped me fix the toys or clean the room, I did that myself. There were only the two rooms on the second floor in this house. My parent's room was downstairs. My brother's room was directly across from mine. My parents rarely came up.

He would try to push me down the stairs. I was terrified of being pushed down the stairs. I would grip the rail with all my might. If he couldn't get me down the stairs he would poke my forehead and say, *just wait, I'll get you.* I would wait until he was at the bottom of the stairs and out of sight before I would let go of the rail. My parents didn't see him try to push me down the stairs; they never seemed to be around, never seemed to see anything.

So I would go to my forest and find a tree. I would climb the tree as high as I could and sit quietly hoping no one would see me. I watched other kids playing in the playground and people walking the paths. They all seemed different from me. They were together, they laughed, and they were not hated. I was bad. That's why I was hated. I didn't know what made me so bad or why I was even born. It seemed wrong somehow, to be born just so that you could be hated. I couldn't understand it.

My father had an art studio in the basement; in the evening my father was often downstairs working on his latest creation. He painted landscapes mostly and he used oil paints and canvass to create beautiful works of art. I enjoyed watching him paint. He would describe to me what he was doing as he went along; "I'm creating layers," "I'm shadowing", or "I have to apply the paint more thinly here". I would listen and watch intently impressed by his explanations and talent. Once he allowed me to help paint a portion of the sky and I felt very important to the painting. We had his work hanging on our living room walls as did all of our relatives. He gave his paintings away to family and friends and sold some at art exhibitions. His brush strokes were confident and sure. He would let me stay with him for a while and then he would say, *Time for bed young lady, up to your room.*

I have no idea where my mother was. It seemed to me that she was hardly ever around. She hated me too; maybe not as much as the brute. She didn't try to kill me but I was rarely allowed in her presence. She would shoo me out of the kitchen, living room or any room that she was in. The most interaction I had with her on a daily basis was to bring her morning tea before leaving for school. I did my best each morning to make her tea just right so that maybe she would be happy with me. It seemed to me she never was.

It was while on this base that I began to consciously feel alone, abandoned and unloved. I was in grades three, four and five while on this base. I would cheerfully say, *Bye Mom* or *Bye Dad* when I was leaving the house. I realized nobody ever answered me. It was as if they did not care whether I came or went. I tried an experiment. I left the house after bed time to see if anyone noticed. Nobody did. I stopped calling out *bye* and just came and went silently. I wasn't sure why nobody cared about me; I was not sure why I was with them. I would find a tree and sit quietly talking in my head to God wondering why I was alive and what I was supposed to do. Then I would find a bird, wounded in some way. I would pick it up and bring it home. I would find a box and make a safe place for the bird to heal. I would do what I could to help it heal. It made me feel good when I was able to bring the bird back to my forest and release it to fly again. Something in that gave me hope. Hope that maybe one day I could fly away and heal from my broken wing.

I loved this particular base. I swam and tap danced and learned bowling. Every Friday night the rec center gym was made into stations and we had free play station to station. The trampoline was set up, the uneven parallel bars, the parallel bars, the vaulting horse, wrestling on mats, a climbing ladder from floor too ceiling, so much fun. I was one of the few who could make it to the top, and the only girl who dared. We had badminton nets set up and leaders playing games in the middle like hot potato with small bean bags. So much fun on Friday night. Swimming was the last activity. What a way to end the day, the week, with my favorite.

On Saturday mornings we had bowling for one hour, swimming for one hour, gymnastics and so on; a whole bunch of organized activities in different parts of the rec center and we went from one to the next to the next. How I loved sport and recreation. Like being in the trees, I was free because my brother was not there.

In grade four my father had a heart attack. It was serious. We thought he would die. He was sent to a military hospital. There were many adjustments for the family to make. I think it was at this point that the pressures of life began to become insurmountable for my parents. Besides changing his lifestyle, his diet and exercise routine, I later learned that this medical condition prevented my father from ever being promoted in the armed forces again. He had served his country twenty-two years. He was only 38 years old.

He was detachment commander on this base and the previous base and I knew that he was an important man. He held a high security clearance and his job included decoding secret messages. He held an insignificant rank yet was respected for his leadership, communication and training skills. Many of his staff who came to visit said he was the best at his job and they aspired to be like him.

He got a call at work one Friday telling him his next promotion had come through; he would be receiving it on Monday morning. On Saturday he had his heart attack and his promotion was withheld. After the heart attack, due to the damage to his heart he was deemed medically unfit to receive his promotion. He was told that he would never be promoted again. He served the remainder of his military career watching as all of the men he trained so well bypass him in the ranks.

Through listening to my Dad talk with other military men I learned a lot about respect for the uniform and the people who wear it. I learned about levels of authority and how to respect authority. We had men from all ranks visit our house. My father gave each of them their due respect but there was electricity in the air when men of higher rank were visiting-especially generals. My father was fond of saying, *you may not be able to respect the man but you always respect the uniform. Always respect the rank. You may not always like the decisions made by those in authority but always follow your orders.* My father had to make many changes to his lifestyle after his heart attack. He quit smoking, started exercising more and made many unwelcome changes to his diet. We were told it was important for him to avoid stress.

I was aware that both my parents liked to drink and whisky was the favorite. When pressures mount, the bottle becomes a friend able to suspend reality even if only for a few fleeting hours. Evenings were spent in such a way by the adults at our house.

Meanwhile, upstairs, my brother had progressed to pushing me up against the wall by the throat with one hand and fondling my breasts with the other, touching me down there. *Don't say a fucking word, or I'll kill you, bitch.* I was eight years old. He had been coming into my room at night after I had been sent to bed, after the drinking started and he was doing things I knew were very bad, very dirty things. He would touch, poke, lick private places; very bad things. *You like it when I do this, you want me to do this. I can tell because you're always in your room waiting for me to come.* I never made any sound while these things were happening. I stayed very still but when it was over and he left my room I would start to shake in fear knowing how dirty and bad I really was and that it must be the reason my mother hated me.

I wanted to scream, *No I don't. I don't like it, I don't want it.* I was too afraid to say it and not sure if it was true. Why would he do it if I didn't want it? Why didn't I scream?

I tried to hide under the bed, holding my breath. I saw his legs walking towards me and then his face, so fast in front of me, it scared me to death. *There you are, come out.* I came out from under the bed and then we were on top of it.

I did run away. Three times I ran away before my father had his heart attack. Every time I tried to run away, I was caught by the military police. Once I made it off base and hid under a bridge. MP's are not supposed to police off the base but they were sent by someone to find me. They were not kind or gentle when they found me. They grabbed my arm and told me that I could go to jail for running away. They told me that jail is a bad place where little girls can *get hurt. You don't want to go there, they say. We better not ever have to find you again because we won't be bringing you home next time.* Today I realize that by this point, I was now the one causing the biggest trouble for my parents. My brother's behavior problems stayed in the house; but when I ran away I involved others. *You're a troublemaker,* my mother said after the police brought me back.

When my father was in the hospital after his heart attack and we were not sure that he would make it; we were told not to create stress for Dad. Stress could kill him. Try not to upset your father the doctor said. I did not try to run away again after that. I vowed I would never run away again. I did not want to be a troublemaker.

I wanted to be good. I tried to be good. I tried to be good at school and I was one of the best at reading. I was one of the fastest when doing our schoolwork and I rarely made mistakes. I tried to be good to broken winged birds; I tried to be good at monkey bars and catching frogs and climbing trees. I tried to be good at brownies, bowling, swimming, gymnastics, skating. I tried to be good at staying out of the way and making morning tea just right. I tried to be good at cleaning my room, but none of those things mattered because I was not good. I was a very bad little girl who should not have been born. I deserved to be hated and deserved to be hurt.

The base priest gave me a small bible, the New Testament and I read it. I underlined some lines with my blue colored pencil, the lines that I liked; the ones Jesus said. I wanted to be like Jesus who was good. In my treetops I often talked to God and asked him to help me to be a good girl. Every Friday night and Saturday morning I would put my troubles away for a while having fun at the gym and in the pool.

On Wednesday evenings we had catechism class and after I got home I was allowed to watch the Bionic Woman on TV. Her name was Jamie. She was part normal and part machine. She had strength and super hearing in one ear and a dog named Max. Max was a German Shepard, my favorite kind of dog. Jamie was beautiful and nice. She helped people and I wished she was my mother. Many times I dreamed that she was.

German Shepard's were my favorite kind of dog because I got to see them in action during dog shows on the base. At a command the dogs would come out with their trainers and men in padded suits. Fifteen or more would line up side by side in a row. Sitting at attention, ears pointing straight up, not moving a muscle, not making any sounds, just waiting. The guys in the padded suits lined up too across from the dogs as far away as the length of a swimming pool. And everybody waited, not moving, staying silent and still until the command.

When the command came, it was amazing to see as so many dogs take off running at once; as fast as they could towards the men in the suits, some grabbing an arm with their teeth and others knocking down some of the men. All the dogs kept up their attack and did not stop until the command came to stop. Each dog obeyed the command in unison and immediately returned to sit by their trainer.

The dogs did other tricks too, I saw an obstacle course where they went under things or jumped over things. They climbed slanted boards, picked things up and dropped them. They laid on their bellies and inched forward, sat, barked; all on command and in unison. These dogs reminded me of military men.

The air shows were an awesome display as well. This base was an air force base and the roar of planes could be heard night and day. The shows were spectacular and you could go into the planes and see where the pilots sat. The history of each craft was told by the pilot who stood beside his plane. An announcement was made signalling the flight show and just like the dog show, many planes in unison doing tricks in the air. Spinning, twirling, diving and rising. Flying in pattern like a flock of geese. The sounds and the smell of the show stayed with me long afterwards.

I carried them with me, the dogs, the planes and the bionic woman. Into my dreams to help ward off the feeling of badness that plagued me at night. I tried so hard during the day to be like the dogs, smart and obedient. I tried to be like Jamie Somers who was helpful and kind. I dreamt of being like the birds and the planes, able to fly away.

We moved again and I began grade six on another Canadian base. The violence in the home had spread towards my parents. My brother had grown physically big and strong. When people see him they remark, "He's a big boy. He should play football. He'll be a linebacker one day." My brother fought with my father. Real blows. The same man we're supposed to keep from stress. My father was the man with the heart condition and stress could kill him. My brother would punch him and make him bleed. I was constantly afraid that my brother's episodes would trigger another heart attack. I was afraid my father would die. If my father died I would be left with a mother who barely acknowledged my existence and a brother who hated me.

The first rape took place on this base. I have no idea where my parents were. I was in my room and it was still light outside. My brother flew in the door so fast. I was hit, pushed and on the floor before I knew what was happening. He pinned my body to the floor with his weight and I couldn't move. He was lying on top of me and his face was directly in front of mine. He held one elbow above my head; my other arm was pinned beneath his body. He actually tried to kiss me. I was repulsed. I shook my head from side to side but he kept putting his lips on mine. I thought I would puke. I tried to wriggle, tried to kick, tried to scream. He screamed, "Shut the fuck up, shut up, shut up, shut up"! He put both hands around my neck and started choking me. He banged my head off the floor over and over. I stopped struggling. As he raped me he said, *You're mine now, bitch. Now you're mine. I told you I'd get you.* When he was finished he slowly licked the side of my face from the bottom of my throat to the top of my forehead. He got up, pulled up his pants, gave me one swift kick said, *fucking bitch* and walked out of the room.

After he left I was not able to move. My body started to shake but I could not get up off the floor. I don't know how long I stayed there. Tears streamed out of my eyes but I was silent. I was nine years old. I had no idea what just happened. I only knew it was very bad.

This was to be my life for the next seven years.

This base was not like the other base's I lived on. The base was not self-sufficient or self-enclosed. It did not have its own school or rec center or grocery store. I started grade six in the village elementary school. The principal was from Pakistan. He was my homeroom teacher also. I could barely understand him. I found grade six hard. Kids didn't walk single file in the hallway like my other schools. They walked in all directions like chaos and bumped into each other. Mostly on purpose. Kids were meaner. Unlike army brats they had friends for a long time and kept with that group. On base's that doesn't happen. On base's, friends come and go; sometimes with very little warning. You learn to make friends quickly and easily. You learn to let them go. On base's everybody lives in the same kind of PMQ. Nobody thinks they are better than anybody else because they live in a bigger house.

It was a big change. I was scared at recess and lunch. Nobody stood in line and took turns on swings or slides. They pushed you off or said mean things. They threatened to hurt you if they were bigger or if they were boys.

The best thing about this base for me was Friday night. On Friday night the hangar was open for us and we got to shoot a 22 caliber rifle at paper targets. The price was ten bullets for a dollar. My allowance at the time was two dollars. You could get a bag of chips, a can of pop, a chocolate bar and a pack of gum from the base canteen for a dollar. Most of the kids used one dollar for treats and one dollar for target practice. I didn't care about the treats very often; I usually took twenty shots. It was fun and gave me something to focus on. I could beat a lot of the kids, especially the boys who I was starting to hate. It made me smile to be better than them.

I had swimming too, only we had to drive to town to get to the pool. I was almost finished all my levels. I was working on my last swimming badge.

I was not raped everyday. He would look directly at me, lick his lips slowly and say, *Tomorrow you're mine.* I knew what that meant. The anxiety of waiting until tomorrow or trying to find a way out was as bad as the event itself. The words that were spoken to me became more and more vile. I was called every name in the book. I was told that I liked it rough and that I wanted to be raped. At one point I learned that fighting only gets you hurt worse. That lesson came after an incident with a knife to the throat when I was twelve. I stopped fighting altogether after that.

Over a period of years, I learned to do what I was told in order to avoid more violence. If told to remove my clothing, I did so. Whatever I was told to do, I did. I did not try to protest or fight. I followed orders. Besides feeling the guilt and shame which naturally come to all victims of assault, I began to feel a self-hatred so deep and so real it made guilt and shame seem like they are fleeting emotions. I despised life. I despised myself. I knew that I was a filthy, dirty girl. I believed that I was every name that I was called. I believed that it was me who brought this on and that it was my fault. Sometimes I didn't even need the command; when he came to my room I silently took my own clothes off and laid on the floor.

Once, when I got older he wanted a struggle but I tried not to react. *Fight bitch* he demanded. His body was lying on top of mine and he held my wrists to the floor beside my head. I kept telling myself, don't react, don't react, don't react. *Fight you fucking bitch.* I felt a squishy thing on my thigh. He used his body weight as a weapon. He gave up and got off me with a final thrust to my wrists, a kick to my side. He called me the name and left the room. My non reaction had worked for me. The second time I was not so lucky.

He had me in the same position lying on the floor, still using his body weight as a weapon, cutting off my ability to breathe. *Fight bitch, fight you fucking bitch, FIGHT!* screaming His spit hit my face. I tried my best not to react. He started pinching and biting. He was cutting off my air and it was hard to breathe. *Awe, come on!* He said as if it were a game. At that moment he lifted his body weight and I sucked in a deep breath. I made the mistake of moving my head and opening my eyes. He reacted fast and tried to put his lips on mine. I lost it. I started to scream, started to fight, tried to kick my legs, twist my body, get his hands off my wrists, screaming and screaming with tears running down my face in frustration. I couldn't get him off. He laughed as I struggled and said; *now we're having fun. You like it rough, you like being raped; you filthy fucking whore.* It ended the same way it always did. He got up, kicked me, laughed, called me the name and left the room.

I was sobbing, crying and shaking. Everything hurt, especially my wrists. I was so frustrated with myself for losing control. *If only I had not reacted.* I was weak, pathetic. A psycho. Unable to maintain control of myself. I was disgusted with me. As I got up from the floor I noticed sticky goo on my belly. Not knowing or caring what it was, it was just part of my filth. I needed to clean up.

For him it was a game. He decided what version of the game we would play. He decided when we would play. He decided how long the game would last. He made up the rules as he went along. I learned to play the game and to follow the rules.

In public I was appeared to be a normal, happy girl. I was. It was part of the game, being normal on the outside. Not letting anyone see. I knew I had to be just as good at that. I learned how to put away all of the ick and to find beauty and happiness in sport, in school, in friends, in books and in nature. I could always find a way to make someone smile or laugh., I made it my daily mission. I was successful with it. I was satisfied with my contribution of good to the world. I was helpful, I was likeable. One teacher told me; "although not particularly humorous, you do have a sharp wit". That made me laugh. I considered how to expand on my not particularly humorous humor. I still smile at that one.

Laughter is the best medicine.

While attending university my friend and I wanted to see the stand-up comics at a local club. The ticket price exceeded our entertainment budget. When the club announced an opportunity to win free tickets I was all in. The contest was simple, tell a joke on stage; if you get the most applause for the funniest joke, you win the tickets.

When I first heard of the contest I knew I had to win it. I combed every possible source for jokes that week. When the night of the contest came, I was the last to go up on stage. I knew I would win and I did. In the third week, the comedian who followed commented that I should be the one getting paid. He thanked me for warming up his audience. It feels good to help people laugh. It feels good to help people feel good, even if only for a moment or two. My childhood goal was a good one. I remain committed to it and proud of it.

I knew I was good at showing my happy face.One summer I was at a campground. There was a pool at this campground so that's where I spent my time. While swimming an older boy touched me down there as he swam past. I did not react in any way. He did it again a few more times, touching other parts as well. He and two others asked me to follow them to their tent; they had something cool to show me. I followed along hoping it was a puppy. Once inside the tent the tone changed to one that I was familiar with and I got scared. I did not run and I did not fight. I did not make a sound. I just let the boys carry out their intention. My brother wasn't even there. Nobody said vile words to me during this episode but they didn't have to. The vile words were already in my head. I said them to myself. I wanted this to happen, I liked it when it happened and I brought it on myself because I was a filthy whore. I was eleven years old.

The violence I experienced at the hands of my brother would come on so fast. One moment he could be walking by like normal and the next moment-bam, I was hit, kicked, slapped or punched. There was no notice, no time to prepare. I was always shocked. I'm not sure why. I came to expect an attack at any moment and I was always on guard but every time he smacked me or kicked me I was shocked. I couldn't believe what was happening. I couldn't believe it was happening every day and I couldn't believe everybody else pretended not to notice.

Many people witnessed physical attacks against me by my brother. Nobody said anything or tried to stop him.

While things were happening to my body, I was able to go somewhere else in my mind. It became easy for me to enter into a world of fantasy where I was swimming in the ocean, lying on the beach or flying through the sky instead of being in the moment that I was actually in. This mental strategy became helpful to me later on in life.

My father retired from the military and we moved to a small town in eastern Canada. It was the summer before I started grade eight. My parents were more and more controlled by my brother. They favored him in every way trying to appease the episodes. I got a job at the local swimming pool as a junior lifeguard and swim teacher assistant. After I got the job I was required to provide for my own needs. School clothes, supplies and personal items were not provided by my parents. They provided all these things and more for my brother. He would demand with violence the things he desired and they succumbed to his demands every time. One time my brother received Nike sneakers that cost $150.00. I complained to my mother that it was not fair. "You're the mature one", she said. "You understand".

I did understand. I resented it but I did understand. I understood that he drained them of everything they had. All of their resources were used up on him; physical, mental, emotional and financial. They had nothing left for me. They were doing the same thing as I was-surviving. All the while projecting the image of a good catholic family.

My mother was working in the cafeteria at the local hospital and my father was managing the local Legion. Both were hard workers and did their jobs well. We were in church every Sunday, mom liked bingo and dad contributed to the community in a variety of ways.

On weekends my mother's family would visit. The adults would sit around the table playing scat, a favorite card game. Reminiscing, gossiping, and playing to win. It became a regular sight to find an uncle sleeping on the couch or on a mattress in the living room. They were an interesting set of siblings; sounding especially odd in their half made up half French Acadian language. If they didn't know the French word for an object they wanted to describe they either made one up or said the word in English with a pseudo French accent. It was funny to listen to them talk. I couldn't understand some of the words they used but they seemed to have no difficulty understanding each other. It seemed to be everyone's right to come into a sibling's house visit for a while and take whatever you fancied as you left. My mom had a ceramic German Sheppard dog that I particularly liked but so did an aunt who simply took it one day saying it would look better at her house. Back and forth it went, nobody asking just saying I'm taking this and leaving with whatever they pleased.

They ate well, large meals that always included homemade pickles and chow. The women and men created fish chowders and assorted fish dishes, rabbit pie, rabbit stew, deer dishes and moose meat. They told stories of eating porcupine that their father found on the side of the road when they were kids. I thought they were totally gross, especially when they fought over who got to eat the rabbit eyeballs.

Playing cards for money and combining it with alcohol could produce arguments and disputes between the siblings. My mother often said; "life's too short to fight." Her words put an end their arguments easily especially after she got sick. She was the glue that kept them together.

I received two hamsters as a gift one year. They were in a cage that we got from an uncle. It was a cage for rabbits; it was too big for hamsters. A couple of weeks after receiving them, the hamsters were fighting in the cage. They could be noisy. It was not the first time that the hamsters had fought. The high pitched squeals that they made while fighting bothered my brother.

He burst into the room, grabbed the cage and was beating me with it before I realized what was happening. I didn't have time to think. I just covered my face and head as best I could with my arms. I was huddled in a ball against the wall. He stopped when he spent his energy. He was breathing hard as he tossed the cage to the floor. My hamsters were dead.

I was shocked again. Sawdust shavings and tiny spots of hamster blood were on the floor and the wall. I knew nobody would help me clean it up. I knew my brother would not get into any trouble for what he had done. It was my fault for not keeping the hamsters quiet. I did not know what to do with the dead hamsters. I was sad because they were dead. I left my room to go get cleaned up and calm down. I don't know what happened to my hamsters or what became of the cage. The cage was gone when I came back to my room. I never saw it again. I went to the living room where my father was sitting in a chair reading the newspaper, "Where is my hamster cage and where are my hamsters" I asked. My father flipped down one corner of the newspaper and said, "I don't know what you're talking about". Then he simply flipped the corner of the newspaper back up. I encountered the brick wall of denial again. He was the only other person home. Knowing denial was impenetrable I turned and walked back to my room. If not for a few bits of sawdust and a couple of tiny dots of blood left on the wall, I would have thought I made it all up and had never owned hamsters in the first place. I picked up the few remaining bits of sawdust and wiped away the tiny spots of hamster blood that had splattered onto the wall, in shock, wondering how my father could not have heard, and wondering who had taken away the cage and the mess.

One edge of the cage had clipped the corner of my eye and the eye went black. I was embarrassed by the black eye. It wasn't a bad one but it was noticeable. As a cadet I was to be carrying the Canadian flag in the Remembrance Day parade that weekend. I told my father that I couldn't carry the flag with my eye like that. *I don't see a black eye* I remember looking in the mirror thinking *there really is something wrong with you. You see things that are not there.* Over and over I looked at my reflection willing myself not to see the black eye until I no longer saw it. I felt better after that. I felt like maybe I wasn't a psycho. My father was right; I didn't have a black eye.

On parade morning, the first cadet I saw said to me, "What happened to your eye?" I was stunned to hear the question. "There's nothing wrong with my eye" I said. I turned and walked away.

I was never sure after that whether what I saw or experienced was ever real. I thought I must be what he said I was- a psycho bitch. He always said if I ever told anybody they would never believe a psycho like me. I believed him. I was very confused. Maybe I made the whole thing up or maybe I didn't. Somebody noticed the eye but not my dad. I had looked at my eye in the mirror until I saw the black eye wasn't there. How could I have done that if the black eye was there? That alone seemed crazy to me and sure proof I could not trust myself. My brother was right; I was a psycho. He always said that he was going to kill me. I believed him about that too.

I took to locking myself in the bathroom when my parents were not home. It was often that they were out. My mother liked Bingo and she attended many games. My father had work or meetings or he was teaching something to someone or someone needed him for something. I was left to fend for myself. When my parents came home to find me locked in the bathroom they would ask my brother why. He would tell them that he didn't know. He said that I was a freak, a psycho; something was wrong with me, a mental case he would say because I locked myself in the bathroom for no reason.

My parents never asked me why. In my heart I said *on the day that they find the courage to ask me why I lock myself in, I will find the courage to tell them the reason.* The day never came.

I was hopeful once when I was told we were going to see a family counsellor. I thought my chance to be saved had come. I thought surely the counsellor will ask me why I lock myself in the bathroom. I purposed myself to tell why. I was excited for the day of the appointment to come. Finally, I would have the chance to tell what was happening to me and someone would help me. I thought I was saved.

We drove to the counsellor's office together. Nobody said a word in the car. When we were called into the office, the counsellor greeted my parents and shook their hands. He said hello to me and my brother. My parents and I sat together on a couch and my brother sat beside us on a chair. There was some small talk between the adults. My brother said something about hockey. Soon the counsellor said, "I guess we're here to talk about why Victoria locks herself in the bathroom." I held my breath. My heart was pounding in anticipation. One by one he asked every member of my family why I locked myself in the bathroom. The counsellor did not look at me once while he was asking them. Each one of them replied in turn that they did not know why I locked myself in the bathroom. He did not ask me. He asked each one of them a second time if they were sure they knew of no reason why I would lock myself in.

Each one said they were sure they knew of no reason. The counsellor said, "Well, I guess we will not be able to solve this today." The counsellor thanked us for coming and we left the office.

I couldn't believe what had happened. I was stunned again. I was shattered. I was incensed. My chance had been lost. *He didn't ask me. He didn't ask me!* I couldn't believe he didn't ask me. I cried myself to sleep for weeks. My chance had been lost. I knew I would never get another chance. I understood that nobody really wanted to know. I encountered the brick wall of denial again and it seemed to be everywhere.

We never returned to his office again.

One time I was visiting at a cousin's house and my cousin and I were sitting on the back deck enjoying the sun. My brother came out of house and kicked me as hard as he could. My cousin was outraged because he was wearing steel toed boots. She made a big deal out of it and started to call for her mother. "Don't bother" I said. "It won't do any good". I had no hope that anyone would ever help me. "Yes, it will," she said. "My mother will do something". My aunt came out onto the deck and my cousin told her what happened. I never knew whether my aunt discussed the incident with my parents. Nothing changed for me.

If you were to ask me which thing was the worst I experienced, I would say it was the assaults that took place in a crowded room in three seconds or less. Witnesses all around but nobody sees anything. We could be at a family function or in a school gym filled with kids and he would walk by and just grab a body part quickly. He always had that evil grin on his ugly face. He enjoyed tormenting me. This game was like a game of cat and mouse and I tried to know where he was at all times in order to avoid him. I was not always successful as being in groups of people make it more difficult to track the whereabouts of one person. Other people don't know there is a game going on, they don't realize they block your view or capture your attention by engaging in conversation. There seemed always to come a moment when the cat was able to strike. These assaults incensed me. I would have to leave wherever I was. No matter how hard I tried to hide it I was visibly upset. "What's wrong with her" people would ask. My brother always had the answer, "psycho-freak".

After every cat and mouse game I was determined to make someone smile or laugh. I was determined to make someone else feel good. It made me feel good about myself. Of all the games my brother and I played I hated cat and mouse the most. In my heart I kept this thought, *I win*.

The house we moved to when we retired was our first civilian home and the first home my parents owned. In this house, I got the big room. There seemed always to be one bedroom bigger than the other. In every PMQ, I got the small room, in our home; the big room was mine. I was told that my parents were building a room in the basement for the brute and I could hardly wait until the room was finished and ready. I was happy not to be so near him.

In the floor just outside the door to my room was a grate. My father had a hole cut through the floor boards and had the grate put in so heat could travel up from the basement. While living in his basement room, one of my brother's favorite games was stab your sister in the feet with the steak knife. He would hide, wait for me to open my door and then shove the knife blade through the slots in the grate into the bottom of my feet. The first time he stabbed my foot I fell. It hurt. I was bleeding but the cut was small. I did my best to fight back any tears that tried to form and refused to limp or baby the foot.

Just a new game in the torment your sister repertoire we had formed. He changed weapons frequently after I learned to hop over the grate. He tried everything from forks to sewing needles, darning needles, knitting needles, and thin pieces of wood. As I hopped higher his weapon got longer trying to reach me.

The steak knife was his favorite and if he could surprise me, or if I forgot to hop; the knife did the most damage.

Every time he got me he would laugh. It was funny to him when he caused me to fall. My habit became to open the door and immediately look down. The glint from the knife blade and his ugly face were often there. I wondered how the heck he could always be there. No matter the time, day or night his ugly face was always there. I hated his ugly face. I despised the wicked grin. I thought his was the ugliest face in the whole world.

I was starting to become tired of playing games.

CHAPTER THREE

Fortifying Insignificance

I told my father that my brother
had molested me

I became obsessed with killing myself. I thought it was the only way I could end my misery. I am very visual so I would try to conjure up an image of me killing myself. There was always whisky at home and my father had pills for his heart. I thought I could drink the whisky and swallow the pills. I got the whisky bottle from under the kitchen sink and went to my Dad's dresser where the pills were. I tried to grab the bottles of pills but as I reached for them I could hear was my father's voice saying, *Promise me you won't ever touch the pills on top of my dresser.* I couldn't touch them. Since that idea was not going to work I thought maybe I'll drown myself. This thought did not last long. I knew I could not drown myself. I love the water. I was a fish in water. I could hold my breath for a long time and I was so accustomed to breathing properly for swimming that I knew I would not be able to kill myself by drowning. I thought to use a knife to slit my wrists. I couldn't visualize that one either. I was afraid of knives since knife day.

Knife day happened when I was twelve. By that time, I was used to being slammed and held by the throat up against a wall. This day my brother used his whole body to pin me to the wall just outside my room and held the butcher knife to my throat. "You better do exactly as I say or I'll shove this fucking knife so far up your fucking cunt you'll feel the blade in your throat" he threatened.

He motioned with the knife for me to go in my room and told me to get on my knees. He took down his pants and sat on the edge of the bed. "Suck it" he said. I was confused. I didn't have time to think before he grabbed the back of my head and forced it towards his groin. *Put it in your mouth and suck it.* I ended up gaging and puking into my green trash can that was stamped DND on the bottom. I thought he peed in my mouth. I wondered, *Where does he come up with this stuff?*

Desperate for a solution I thought I'd throw myself in front of a truck on the highway. I can't tell you how many times I was on the side of the highway in the dark waiting for a transport truck. Sometimes I would be there for hours waiting for a truck to come and no truck would come. Sometimes a truck would come and I could not do it. The last time I tried it was fight day; I was determined, it was raining and after chickening out again I walked home soaking wet, sobbing quietly letting the rain wash away my tears. The truth was I didn't want to die I just wanted my misery to stop. The truth was I didn't really want to kill myself. Killing myself was just not the right solution to my problem. After about a year with this truck obsession I accepted the fact that I was not going to kill myself. I made a vow to myself that I never would. I was fifteen years old.

In an attempt to escape my life for a little while, I decided I would get drunk. I decided on Friday evening to attend a social event with some of my older lifeguard friends at the local university. The senior lifeguards had a habit of having liquor delivered to the back door of the pool at closing time. I asked one friend if I could add to the order. There was a band playing at the student union building and we were to have a few drinks in one of the dorms before going to dance. For my drinking pleasure I decided on a micky of vodka. This was my first experiment with alcohol. Not knowing how to drink responsibly, I downed the entire bottle as fast as I could. I don't remember much from the rest of the evening.

I do remember vomiting out of the third floor window of the dorm and my friend telling me that they were leaving the dorm to head over to the dance. I was passed out in the room, the owner of the room, a friend and co-worker said I should stay put. Later, I heard my friend tells me that he was putting me in the room next door. I was in the way. He had a girl coming. I do not remember being moved. I woke slightly to find a male on top of me. I had my paycheck from the pool in cash in my pocket. I said, "Please don't take my money". He said "It's not your money I want". I went back to sleep. In the morning, I pulled up my pants, left the building and walked across the rugby field to work. Inside my heart I knew I did wrong by drinking and by putting myself in a place that I had no business being in. It was my fault that I had been violated again. This night saved me from a lifetime of addiction to alcohol or drugs because I vowed that morning never to lose control like that again.

After work the next day, my friend from the dorm commented that the neighbor would like to see me again. At first I was greatly offended but after some thinking I thought I could possibly erase the shame of what I had done if this guy became my boyfriend. If he was my boyfriend it wouldn't be as bad I thought. I went to see him and realized he and I were not interested in the same outcome. He was interested in only one thing and it was not being my friend.

At this time, I had two boys in my group on the swim team that gave me great pleasure as a coach. They had come up through swimming lessons with me and I recruited them for the team. The pleasure came with simply being in their presence, they were cousins who were friends. They were playful and jovial, always had funny stories and they were both adorably cute. Another source of my pleasure was in knowing they were destined to be Olympians. One because he had the skill, talent, and discipline to make it; and the other a competitive nature and determination not to be outdone by his cousin. They were so much fun to watch, to coach and to challenge.

So many of the people I taught to swim gave me great pleasure. Whether they were adults or children I enjoyed helping them learn to love water as I did. I had a set of grandparents once. They had a cottage by the beach. They were both afraid of water and wanted to overcome their fear because the grandchildren were coming of age to swim. The grandparents wanted to swim with the kids. I know this family enjoyed many years of safe, happy swimming at the beach. I am satisfied with that.

I felt content with my contribution to my community. I was part of the youth group, raised money for worthy charitable causes and volunteered my time for a variety of events. I taught lifesaving and lifeguarding, administering oxygen, first aid and aquatic emergency care along with swimming, diving and water safety. I taught citizenship, general service knowledge, effective speaking, instructional techniques and drill in the cadet movement. I did my best to help those around me.

I could have earned a fortune at cadet camp just by shining people's boots. Mine always seemed to be the best polished, like glass. I was held up as an example for others which simply sent them to my dorm asking me to shine their boots, offering money. I felt like I had an inside track since my father had taught me to shine my boots. I was using his kit which held a proper brush and buffing cloth along with superior polish and several well worked in polishing rags. Rather than take the money, I offered to teach them to shine.I came home from school or work more than once during these years to find a trail of blood in the house. One day I found a trail starting at the side door through the kitchen and dining area, across the hall and into the bathroom. The worst part of finding a trail of blood is wondering whose blood it is. Most often it was Dad's blood. Worse than wondering whose blood it is finding out its Dad's blood. For me there is horror in finding out that. My next idea was to kill my brother. I wondered if I really had it in me to kill him. I knew I did.

I tried to visualize how I could accomplish it. I had many different ideas but threw away most of them knowing I could not really pull it off. The only plan I could really see me carrying out was to wait until the middle of the night, grab the bat and bash my brother's head in while he slept. I knew that my first two hits would have to be as hard and fast as I could make them otherwise it would be my head bashed in. If I did it, it would be a fight to death; of that I was sure.

I began to lift weights at the university gym so that I could be as strong as I could be. I started to practice with the bat. I wanted to be sure I could land the hit exactly where I needed it to land. I was very serious. The only experience I had with a bat was from softball games in gym class. I was not very good at hitting the ball in gym class. I knew strength wasn't my problem-aim was.

I had to practice after dark so no one would see me. I went down to the bank of a river not far from our house and I swung the bat above my head as hard as I could. I slammed it into the guardrail. The bat bounced so hard off the guardrail that I lost my balance and nearly fell. I had to figure this out.

I went to the riverbank as often as I could. I took to hitting rocks instead of the guardrail. I chose rocks that appeared to be the same size as my brother's head. I learned to move my grip from the end of the bat closer to the center. I practiced loosening and firming my hold until I had the combination I needed. After mastering that technique, I practiced for speed.

Visualization was a technique we used in swimming, one that I believed aided in mastering a skill or a mindset. I visualized hitting him and visualized blood splattering all over his room in the basement. I visualized him taking the bat from me and bashing my head in. At first I was scared of being bashed with the bat. I knew it would hurt but I hoped only the first few hits would hurt and then I would die. If I did not succeed in killing him, I knew I could not use my arms or do anything to protect my face or head. Doing so may lead to pain and damage but not necessarily death and death was my only goal. It did not matter to me who died -him or me;

I was preparing myself for either outcome. If I did succeed I knew I would go to jail for murder. I thought a lot about going to jail. I thought about whether I could handle being in jail. I visualized being in jail. After a few weeks of thinking about it I thought I could handle it. I felt jail was worth it. If I had to stay in jail for the rest of my life it would be worth ending his life and my misery. I thought I could tell the judge why I killed him and maybe I wouldn't have to stay in jail forever. I wasn't afraid of jail; I didn't think it would be any worse than how I was living and I would never have to see him again. I did have one fear; I was afraid that once I started hitting him with the bat, I would not be able to stop. I thought I might like to watch his blood splatter all over the walls and the floor just like he did to my hamsters. I even thought that the only way I could be stopped was to be shot by the police. Even that outcome was fine with me.

These thoughts of killing my brother consumed me for the better part of a year. Many people who knew me during this time thought I was a normal teenager. Some people called me successful as a teen. My grades were good, I was working and volunteering in the community. I was a cadet. I did drama and I was on the student council. My friend's parents often commented to me that they wished their teen was as mature as I was. I had parents of other kids who were getting into trouble come to me for advice.

Nobody knew that I had murder in my heart and mind.

By my own guesstimate I was about two weeks away from carrying out my plan. I was almost ready. I had spent the best part of a year getting ready. I knew I could do it. I knew I had the guts to do it. I felt strong enough to do it. I knew I only had to tap into my rage, push aside any fear and I could do it. Every day with every threat, assault or attack; I was getting closer and closer to murdering my enemy. What pushed me to the edge was what came next.

One night, I found myself in the same position on the floor with him and his ugly face on top of me pinning my body with his and holding down my wrists. He grinned and said, "Beg!"

I was shocked and confused again, "Fuck me" … "Say it!" he ordered. "Say- Fuck me". "Say it!" he screamed in my face over and over; I wouldn't. "Say it you fucking bitch or I'll slit your throat! "I wish I had said, "Slit my throat" but I didn't. *Fuck me* I said weakly.

I watched his face change in front of me. The grin turned sadistic and dark eyes became evil. The creepy sadistic evil face paused for a moment, smiled and spoke again; "Say please".

He waited as though he knew he had to. Waiting for the lump in my throat to clear, watching my internal struggle as tears began to well up in my eyes while I struggled not to let one fall. He waited using his body weight for pressure slowly adding more and more as the tears I could not hold back started to fall from my eyes.

My voice was barely audible *Please.*

The evil sadistic look on his face started forming a slow wide grin, "Please what?"

It waited for my response allowing for the pause that turns contempt and fear into submission.

Please fuck me. "Oh, yeah!" he said as he started thrusting. "I know what you want you fucking whore, I have what you want, I'll give you what you want; say it!" And so this rape went…with me begging over and over and him saying vile words and trusting violently until he was finished, got up, put on his pants, kicked me, called me the name and left my room.

I cannot describe how I felt; I could not on that day, nor can I today. There are no words that fit.

In the morning on the next day;

I was ready to murder him.

It was now a matter of which day I would decide to do it. It wasn't a matter of which day I would kill him; any day was good for that. I only needed to decide on which day I was prepared to go to jail.

I was trying to decide between a Monday and Friday. If I went to jail on Monday I could begin my sentence at the start of the week. I wondered if it may be better to go to jail on Friday and start my sentence on the weekend. Since I couldn't decide between the two I thought about splitting the difference and killing him on Wednesday. Thursday was my favorite day of week and the more I thought about Wednesday the more I liked the choice. If I bashed my brother's head in the middle of the night on Wednesday, I could start my first day of jail on my favorite day of the week. I could start my sentence with two week days and two weekend days. This was a good compromise and a perfect choice I thought. It was a Tuesday when I made this decision so I thought it best to wait until the following week to sit with my decision for a bit and put some things in order first. The decision was made, the next Wednesday it was.

On Saturday in swim class was the cutest little boy. He was in the red level where the kids are just learning to do a front swim. This boy was good. I knew he could swim across the whole width of the pool, fifteen meters. He was only required to swim seven meters to get his badge but I knew he could make the width. He would get scared half way across and would lose his focus and start to sink. Then he would be looking for me to take hold and support him while he caught his breath before starting the way back.

I was always careful to be there at the exact moment any kid in swim class was looking for support. I did not want any child to have fear of the water so I paid very close attention. However far they swam I had them look back and see it. "Look how far you made it", I would say. I always enjoyed seeing the smile on their little faces when they looked back.

On this Saturday I was determined that this little boy would make it all the way across the width. I wanted him to succeed before I went to jail. As he stopped half way across looking for me I took a step back in the water and said, "come to me, I'm right here". He put his head down and took a few more strokes. He looked for me again, "just a little more, you're almost there". The third time he raised his head, he was at the wall.

"Look, look what you did!" I said excitedly. "Look how far you swam; you made it all the way across!" "I did?" He asked. "Look" I said. That was the moment I wanted to capture in my heart. The look on his face as he realized his accomplishment and broke into a wide smile. "I made it all the way across!" he exclaimed. "Yes", I said, "I knew you could do it! "Good for you, good for you!" As I piggy backed him to the other side I knew I would never again see that look on a child's face. The look of pride in accomplishment coupled with joy. I refused to be sad about it but I wanted to remember what it looked like so I could carry it with me to jail. I knew that I would not be teaching swimming lessons in jail, I wanted desperately to keep the memories within me.

I took in the sights, sounds and smells of the environments around me that Saturday. As I walked to and from the pool by way of my favorite street I noticed how beautiful the street was. Big, beautiful homes with green grass, bushes and flowers lined each side. Trees so large that the branches and leaves from each side came almost together, almost touching in the middle creating an umbrella over the street. It looked like streets I read about in novels. Birds could be heard tweeting and singing. They were especially pretty songs as I walked an empty street to work. I wanted to take it all in and remember it, the smell of the grass, the sound of the birds and the beauty of the street. I counted down the number of times I had left to walk it before going to jail.

On Sunday evening while in my room I heard a commotion and went out to see my father and brother at it again. It was a short episode this time. My brother left the dining area and went downstairs to his room. I have never forgotten this moment. I looked at my father, he was leaning on a dining chair with one hand, he was bleeding from the nose and his bangs had flopped to the wrong side. He flipped his bangs to the correct side, looked me straight in the eye and said to me, "take the bat and go bash your brother's head in".

He was serious in that moment and at that exact moment I knew it was not my responsibility to protect my family. It was Dad's responsibility. My thought was, *I'm not doing your dirty work*. In that exact moment I decided I would not kill my brother. I turned away without saying anything and went to my room.

I felt lighter after deciding not to kill my brother. It was a relief. I didn't realize how heavy, how dark my decision had been. Now I was feeling – lighter is the only word I have for it.

I'm not going to kill me and I'm not going to kill him; what am I going to do?

Being sixteen at this point I realized that I was old enough to run away and no one could stop me. If they sent the police after me I would tell the police, why I ran away. I would tell the police that if they tried to send me back I would kill my brother. I would say it would be better to take me straight to jail and avoid all the trouble.

Nobody could make me go back. I had a job and money; I could pay my own way. I realized I could be free.

It didn't seem fair to me that I had to run away, after all; the brute was the problem; he should be the one to go. I decided to confront my father about it since mom was at bingo.

I went to my father and said, "This has got to stop; either he goes or I go". My father looked at me and said, "You'll have to be the one that goes". "Ok", I said; not really surprised at the response. I was disappointed in my dad. I knew I would go as soon as I figured out where to.

I didn't quite get the opportunity to figure that part out. The next afternoon, a Monday, something in me was different. Monday was usually the day I rushed home to get there before my brother so I could lock myself in the bathroom. This day I decided I was not going to lock myself in. I decided I was going to be a normal teenager and watch TV in my parent's room. As I poured myself a glass of ginger ale I thought about throwing the pop in his eyes if he did anything. I would run.. I went to watch TV. I heard him come into the house. He went downstairs first then he came for me. He grinned when he found me reclining on my mother's bed, *there you are.* He came to the side of the bed and grabbed my left ankle. He pulled my leg towards him. I had the ginger ale ready so I threw the pop into his eyes. I was shocked and stunned for a moment when I realized I had hit the target. He let go of my ankle and put both hands to his eyes. "Aaahhh!" he cried & I knew it stung. *Hurry, run!* I gained just enough space and time to run out the door. I left the house without any shoes or a jacket.

I knew I would never go back. I was done. *So now what?*

I went to the house of my friend and her sister. Their mother answered the door when I knocked. I asked if the girls were home and my friend's mother said they were not. "Come in Victoria" she said. "No thank you. I'll come back when the girls are home". "Victoria" she commanded, "come in". I went into the house and sat on the sofa. "You haven't any shoes on" she said. *I ran out of the house and forgot my shoes.* "Let me call your parents and" *No* I interrupted, *they're not home.* "Your brother was home with you?" she asked me. *Yes* "Well, stay here awhile and I'll call your parents later." *No, it won't do any good. I'm not going back. I'm never going back.*

My friend's mother left the room and came back in a minute with a pair of sneakers and a jacket. "Where will you go?" she asked me. *I'll find somewhere.* "You can borrow these for as long as you need them. When you are finished you can return them to me". *Thank you.* "Don't tell the girls you were here" she said. "We don't want my husband to find out". I understood what she meant because her husband was ex-military and a friend to my father.

I spent the evening walking around town. I grew tired and sat on a lone bench. I lay down on the bench and slept a little. I waited after waking for the pool doors to open. After my morning instead of walking directly to school as I normally would, I walked home first and snuck in the door. I knew nobody would be home that time of the morning so I filled my kit bag with the bulk of my clothes. I got my sneakers and left the house. I walked back to my friend's house. "How are you?" she asked me. *I'm ok. Thank you for loaning these to me, I don't need them anymore.* "Where are you going now?" *I'm going to school.* "That's good" she said.

I did think about telling the authorities. I knew I would destroy my father. I was trying to decide what was right. I did not want to shame or embarrass my father. I knew that telling would destroy his reputation and I did not want to do that. Something in my heart was telling me to protect the work he did. My father was contributing much good to the community.

I called an organization that was newly formed in my town. I met with a lady. I made her swear not tell anybody else and not to write anything down. She agreed. I briefly explained that I was being molested at home by my brother. I wanted to know what would happen if I told the police. She said she would look into it and get back to me.

After a couple of days, she did get back to me. She said she spoke with a lawyer. Because my brother was close to my age a judge might consider it child's play. There would be little consequence for my brother. He would probably not go to jail. I could not see destroying my father and his reputation over child's play. I was incensed again. I did not consider what had been happening to me as child's play. I couldn't believe that a judge would. Something in my heart was telling me, "Protect the work". I knew it meant my father's work; all of his community activism, his work with veterans, his work with youth, teaching religion, cadets, 4-H and art. He made significant contributions to the community and he was well respected. I decided not to tell. I would only bring shame to him and no positive change to me. I was on my own.

I was sleeping outside underneath the football bleachers behind the university athletic center. Inside the center I had a locker because I worked at the pool. I kept a few belongings in my locker. I had shower gear and my toothbrush. It was easy to get to work in the morning and easy to get ready for school after that. It was fall and getting cooler. I was cold and sometimes wet at night. The bleachers were not comfortable for sleeping. I did a lot of walking around.

One of the male university students who swam with us offered me to stay at his place. He had a room at a local motel with two beds. I could have the other one. I wondered whether that would be right. I went to see the local priest who presided over us as youth. He was not available so I spoke to an older priest whom I did not know. I asked him if it would be ok to accept the offer. The priest told me it would be sin if I did. I didn't want to sin so I didn't go. It was now October. It was cold and wet and dark early. I did not have a blanket. I was tired. After a couple of nights in the rain I decided to accept the student's offer. Later that night when the student tried to get into the bed where I was, I found myself running out into the night again. I could hear him calling after me, "I'm sorry, I'm sorry, you don't have to go. I'm sorry, it won't happen again". I did not look back. I wondered if I had a sign on my back that said rape me.

I started to cry. *Was there no safe place? Is every boy the same?* I didn't know where I could go. The rents were so high; I could not afford an apartment. I was getting desperate.

He tried to apologize the next day in the hallway of the athletic center. He had tears in his eyes as he said, "I'm so sorry. I just didn't think; why would you leave home? I'm so sorry".

I knew his apology was sincere but I thought him a wimp for having tears; I said, "Never speak to me again" and I walked away. In truth he had pricked the edge of my secret and I was trying desperately to keep it all contained. If I did not succeed I would fall apart into millions of pieces. I would be like Humpty Dumpty. *All the king's horses and all the king's men, couldn't put Victoria together again.*

I was good at employing this strategy; walk away and never look back. I would block it out of mind, file it away and never think about it again. Which also meant never again acknowledging the person I turned my back on.

On Friday after work I was standing at the rail on the bleachers thinking about my situation when a female colleague saw me. She came over and said, "Victoria, you haven't been yourself lately. Tell me what's wrong". I told her that I had left home, had nowhere to live and that I had been sleeping on the bleachers for the past couple of weeks. My female colleague said I could have her dorm room for the weekend because she was going home for the weekend. That should be safe I thought. It would be warm and comfortable. I was very grateful and accepted the offer. The first night in my female colleague's dorm room was terrific. I had a soft, warm bed and a washroom down the hall. Nobody bothered me at all. The second night was different. A couple of the girls wanted to know who I was and what I was doing there. I did not know how to answer them and I was not comfortable with the questions so I just left the dorm and went back to my bleachers.

That was the problem with having secrets-simple questions threw me for a loop and I separated myself from people in order to avoid them. I felt different from everybody else. Everybody else was normal and I was not. I was a psycho freak.

The next week my female colleague had another idea. Students often rented rooms from the local motel on a monthly basis. The rooms had a small kitchenette with two stove burners, a mini fridge and a small sink. They contained two double beds and a bathroom. My female colleague wanted to live in one of these rooms with her boyfriend without her parents finding out. She thought she could convince her parents to allow her to have a room there because the rent was less expensive than residence fees which they paid for her. Her idea was to ask her parents if she could move into a room with me but she would really live with her boyfriend. We would rent the room in her name and I would live there. I would pay half of the rent and if her parents ever showed up I was to cover for her. What a lifeline she was throwing me! I thought the plan was good and I hoped her parents would go for it. I was hopeful and excited again. I had to contain myself because I still had to wait. She would speak to her parents the following weekend and see if they would agree.

They did. I was saved! I had a place to live. The day I was moving to the room, it was pouring, pouring rain but I was so happy. I said to the rain, "You can pour all you like on me but you will not dampen me today". I was saved. Finally, I was saved!

A friend stole me one fork, one knife, one spoon, one plate, one glass and one bowl from the university cafeteria. Now I could add thief to my list of crimes but it didn't matter to me. I needed what I needed. I couldn't afford to buy what I needed so it had to be taken. I figured that the university would not miss the few items. Another friend took a small pot and pan from her mom's kitchen and her mother never noticed. I had everything I needed. I was safe. I was sixteen and in my last year of high school. After a couple of weeks, I started to relax in my little room.

One night I heard a noise outside at the window. I listened quietly. Fear started to rise up in me as I realized someone was trying to get in the back window. I pushed the curtain away to peek out and I saw the glint of a knife blade and that ugly face! There was only one door and it was already locked. I went into the bathroom, locked the door and crawled into the bathtub. I sat in the middle of the tub hugging my knees to my chest, terrified, fully expecting my brother to make his way in through the door and kill me right there in the tub.

My female colleague found me in there the next morning. I came out when I heard her voice. I told her what happened. She said she would tell her boyfriend. She told me not to worry we would figure something out. Her boyfriend was on the university football team, he had lots of big friends and they would keep watch for me. After she spoke to them and the plan was confirmed I felt better. I felt safer after my brother came back several days later and was confronted by a few of these guys. I knew he would not be back after that.

I ate popcorn mostly. I bought Scobey's brand macaroni and cheese dinner. Kraft was my favorite but at twenty-five cents a box, it was too expensive. I would make half the box one evening for supper; have popcorn the next night and then the other half of the macaroni and cheese on the third night. This was my diet. I ate once a day. I figured I needed vegetables of some kind so on paydays I would splurge and buy a personal size pizza with the works for five dollars. The deal came with a can of pop. The pizza had green peppers, onions and mushrooms. Problem solved.

My closest friend Sarah and I tried very hard to hide where I was living. We knew that if Sarah's mother found out where I was living she would not allow Sarah to be my friend. Neither of us wanted that so I was trying to stay under the radar. I did not tell any adults that I was not living at home. One day I was called to the office at school. There I faced the principal and vice principal. They found out I was living at the motel. They found out because some of my friends from school had beer delivered to my room. My principals said they should call the police.

I begged them not to. Every year at our high school someone had died in a drinking related incident. Kids had been hit by cars on the highway; one friend had tried to walk home after a party and froze to death. Without telling them the reason why I told them that I was not drinking. I promised not to allow anyone to walk home alone. I promised that I would not let anyone drink and drive. I told them that the kids were going to drink either way, whether at my place or in the graveyard behind the junior school. I would keep the kids safe. I pleaded with them not to call the police. I said they would thank me at the end of the year because this could be the first year that nobody died at our school due to drinking. Miraculously, they agreed not to turn me in. They warned me they would be keeping an eye on me and if there was trouble they would call. I was relieved. I warned my friends not to have beer delivered by cab again. It was a very strong warning and it was heeded.

I had not spoken with my parents since leaving home. I knew my mother would not want to speak to me but I held great hope that my dad would. I hoped to see him at cadets. I hoped he would be helpful to me secretly. I was really looking forward to seeing him and hoping for a hug.

Since I left home on a Monday, I missed cadets that night. I had missed the promotion ceremony. I knew that meant embarrassment for my father. I was anxious to see him and hoped he would be relieved to see me. I went to cadets and was very quickly informed that the CO wanted to see me in the office. I was hopeful we would have a personal chat and he would want to know how I was doing. I thought we would strategize some excuse for me missing the week prior and I would be given my promotion and position assignment for the upcoming year.

What I encountered broke my heart and any hope I held of a career in the military. My father addressed me as cadet; a break from formality and custom which was to address cadets by rank and last name. It was his way of diminishing my value to the squadron. He said, "Cadet, you're not in uniform". I replied, "Sir, I have no access to my uniform" which he knew since it was at his house. His tone of voice erased the hope I had that he may have brought my uniform for me. He said, "No uniform, no cadets" implying I should leave. Since he obviously did not bring my uniform for me I knew I would not be provided an opportunity to retrieve it.

I replied, "Sir, I have had to take on an extra shift at work on Monday afternoons, I will not be able to attend in uniform". He said, "No uniform, no cadets". I said, "Sir, there are other cadets who do not wear the uniform and you have given them positions in the office, I was hoping you could do the same for me". His reply was curt and authoritative, "I have no office positions available". "You're dismissed."

The truth was there were a couple of female cadets who refused to wear a uniform and my father created office positions for them, granting them favor as he saw them as less fortunate. The girls often threw it in my face and were bullies to me both inside and outside of cadets. Yet, they were favored by my father and I saw it as him mentoring disadvantaged youth so I didn't hold it against them. I saw it as part of his good work in the community. I was happy for the girls. I remembered my mother's words, "You have more than they do; don't be selfish". When I was dismissed I held it against my mother, believing my father must be doing this in order to avoid having to discuss seeing me with her.

I was heartbroken, stripped of my rank and knew that yet again I had encountered the impenetrable brick wall. I was no longer welcome in cadets. I'm not sure what my face looked like as I tried to mask my hurt, but my father's face was stone like and militaristic. His was the face of a commander and his order was final; "You're dismissed".

I was not going to be able to see my dad every week. The rejection of me was complete. I found out a few weeks later that my parents had told relatives, neighbors and friends that I gave them a lot of trouble and had left home to go and live with a boyfriend. I was cut off from the entire family. I was the black sheep.

One day a number of weeks later I did get a call from my Dad, "Your mother says you look like a shaggy dog-get a haircut!" Click. That was the end of the conversation. I did not even get a hello. I was hurt again but knew I had shamed him and deserved my fate. I obeyed as best I could. I ended up bartering haircuts for swimming lessons from a local stylist. He promised to see me through the year and to do my hair for my graduation. It was the best my hair had ever looked, he was an excellent stylist and became one of those friends who helped see me through a difficult year.

I had to leave my little room at the end of April when the university students finished their year. I found an apartment to sublet from another student which gave me a place to finish my year. I couldn't wait to get the heck out of small town eastern Canada.

That summer I worked at an outdoor pool in a small sailing town on a placement with the Red Cross. The Red Cross had arranged room and board for me and I was paid my regular wage. The pool needed a strong guard and a strong teacher to supervise the staff. They had been experiencing episodes of unruly teens. Break in's and vandalism were occurring after closing. I thought it was a perfect opportunity for me and accepted the offer.

It was late in the summer by the time I heard back from the university I applied to. The program accepted fifty students per year at that time. Over three hundred applied each year. I was overjoyed to be accepted. I went by train to northern Ontario.

Not long after arriving at university I found out that everybody was having sex. In first year I lived in a Catholic dorm building on campus. Even there sex was rampant. In the bars where I worked offers for sex came every shift. I was having trouble with the idea of sex. If a guy tried to get close to me I ended up freaking out, running away and crying. I wanted to be normal and have sex like everybody else. If I left my body and went somewhere else in my mind I knew I could get through anything. I was determined to be cured. I started letting the guys in the bar pick me up and take me wherever they wanted to go. The first time I tried my experiment; when the guy tried to kiss me it was enough to send me running. The second time I tried, the first kiss and the first touch came at the same time freaking me totally. In a panic, I ran.

I thought if I just kept trying the day would come when I would get over it, be cured and be normal.

I thought my plan would work, I figured out how to sidestep lip kissing and to maintain control of myself while being touched. I thought I was making it one step further each time I tried so for me that was progress. Panic, running, self-hate, crying and vomiting followed each attempt. All that aside, it was a good plan. I was sure it would work. After a few attempts with this strategy I had to admit that my plan was not working. It was stupid and I was a freak.

I acquired a new plan. I thought I should choose the guy, seduce him and bring him back to my place. I would have control over the pace of events and then I could make it all the way and be cured. Then I would be normal.

I went to the largest bar in the city. I combed the place and chose a guy. It ended up being easy to seduce him and bring him back to my apartment. Something was different about being the one in control. I found power in it. I made it all the way without crying, freaking out or vomiting. I was cured! I had normal sex; maybe I could be normal.

For two days I was really basking in the feeling of power that came from being the one in control.

Then I found out the guy I seduced was getting married the following weekend. I realized then that there was no cure in what I had done. Something about basking in the false sense of power was wrong.

I was eighteen years old. The man I seduced was forty. There was no coincidence in that, only I didn't realize it at the time.

I stopped all efforts at being normal.

I had the distinct privilege to work with some of Canada's elite athletes and coaches in swimming at university. I learned some very valuable lessons.

I saw with my own eyes how far some people will go to destroy greatness. Usually they are people close to the great one. It is sickening to see envy, jealousy and plotting against excellence.

I have stories I wish I could tell you. I acquired two jobs during my first year of university but after Christmas the second year I ended up moving off campus and took on a third job. Several nights I worked until three in the morning and then had class at eight fifteen. At the pace I was going I burnt myself out. One day I literally crashed. I slept for three days straight and did not even wake enough to eat. After waking on the fourth day it was like a weakness had taken hold of my body. I ate soup and lay on the couch for another two days. I couldn't keep up so I dropped out of school.

I added failure to my growing list of crimes.

One of my jobs was managing a submarine shop downtown. I saw Kenny coming one day from across the street. He looked like a cross between Don Johnson from Miami Vice and Luke Spenser from General Hospital. He had curly blonde hair, blue eyes, a nice smile and a white suit. After that first day he came into the shop, he started coming in every day. He made small talk and chatted easily about current world events and the job he held selling various wares to businesses in the downtown. I loaded the subs he ordered with extra meat and cheese. He said they were the best subs he had ever tasted. After a few weeks he asked me to go for a drink after work.

I went for a drink and we talked. We had some things in common. We were both adopted and we both had traumatic childhoods. As adopted children neither of us had felt that we belonged in our families. As wounded children we identified with each other's fear, shame and feelings of loneliness. It seemed like a lot of connection. We had lots in common.

The day after sharing the drink he came to see me at work but I was home sick. Sometime later that evening he found out where I lived and showed up at my door. I let him in. After that he never left. The company he was working for was leaving town to head to another site. He told me he was in love with me and asked if he could stay with me. I let him move in. Within three weeks he asked me to marry him and I said yes. The night of the proposal was the night things got physical. We were married five months later. I was almost four months pregnant when we married. Shame followed me everywhere. I was nineteen years old.

This was not a marriage made in heaven. Violence began swiftly. The first time he hit me it was a slap on the face. I can't remember what the argument was about or what I said. I just remember the slap. I was not prepared to be slapped in my marriage. I called the police. Two policemen came to the apartment. After telling them what happened they asked me if I wanted to press charges. When I told them that I was not interested in charges being laid they insisted I accompany them to the police station. I was put into a small room. The two officers gave me a lecture about wasting their time. I explained that I only wanted them to tell my husband not to hit me. They were angry with my response. Police officers can be very intimidating. I had no idea that I would make them so angry by calling them. After that they left me by myself in the room for what seemed like a long time. A female officer eventually came in. She said she knew it wasn't the first time I had been hit. She said on average women are assaulted three times before they call the police. She said spousal violence gets worse when the wife is pregnant. She had lots of statistics, facts and reports. I had never heard anything like this before and I could not understand what it had to do with me. I was not a victim of spousal violence. It was the first time my husband hit me. He didn't really even hit me it was only a slap. She encouraged me to press charges. I said I could not. When I was finally able to leave the station that day I vowed never to call the police again.

The day before our son's first birthday I found out my husband was having an affair. I also found out it was the second affair of our short marriage. I was devastated and heartbroken. I felt unlovable. I wanted to leave the marriage. I phoned home. My mother told me that I had made my bed and now I had to lay in it. I wanted to cancel the birthday party because I did not have the heart to celebrate. I phoned my husband's mother and told her of the troubles in my marriage. His mother came to pick me up and she drove me back to her house. I was advised to proceed with the party because there were so many guests invited. I did. I put on my happy face. The next day I was summoned to my husband's Grandmother's house. In her home Grandma told me about her husband. How he too was violent, a drinker, and about his affairs. She explained that men are not able to help themselves because they have no outlet for their emotions. She said I would learn to avoid violence by being pleasing to my husband. We must look the other way when affairs happen she said, expect affairs to happen and just ignore them. She explained that affairs do not mean that the husband does not love the wife. The advice sounded familiar to me. Just ignore it when someone violates you. By this time, I had been married seventeen months. My son was a year old and I was two months pregnant with our second child. I was twenty-one years old. I decided to stay.

I blamed myself. I thought, *if only I were prettier, thinner, smarter, a better cook, kept a cleaner house, was better in bed, something. If only I were something more, maybe then he would love me.* I was very close to my due date and in the shower one day when he came home. To this day I do not know why he was angry. He came into the bathroom and punched into the shower where I was. He got us directly in the stomach. I couldn't believe he did that. He turned around and left the apartment. I was in shock most of the day. I was hoping and praying that my baby was alright. I went into labor that night. When my water broke it was green and sticky. I was alarmed when I saw that. I did not want to make my husband angry so I did not wake him until the morning. I labored all night alone. My aunt had agreed to watch my son while I was in the hospital so when my husband woke in the morning we dropped our son off at my aunt's house first. Then my husband dropped me off at the hospital.

The doctor told me the water was green because of stress to the baby. The baby had a bowel movement while inside He said. It was a tricky situation because the baby would be breathing that fluid and it could possibly interfere with respiration. I never knew if the punch had been the trigger for that stress but I suspected that it may be the case. When our daughter was born it took the nurses several minutes to clear out her mouth and nose. I was very tense and scared hoping that she would cry or make some sound. Eventually the nurses were able to clear her airway and she was breathing. She let out a cry. I was relieved. She was beautiful. I now had a millionaire's family the hospital staff said. They said I was very lucky.

I was not feeling lucky. I was feeling unsure of everything. I was alone and afraid. My daughter and I did not have a single visitor during our hospital stay, not even my husband.

We came home from the hospital three days later. There had been a woman in my apartment, in my bed while I was gone. I know this because he was not shy about telling me. He was mad at me for being back because she had to go. He demanded sex. I couldn't believe what he was asking. I said I couldn't. He said I could. Many people believe that a woman can't be violated by her own husband. I believe something different. A piece of my heart died that afternoon while my beautiful baby daughter slept in her crib a few feet away from the bed where my husband took from me what he felt he was due. My son returned home a couple of hours later excited to see his new baby sister. It was time for the happy face again.

Kenny started taking the keys to the building, the mailbox and the apartment which meant that it was difficult for me to leave the building. The building rule was that you were not allowed to buzz the super if you forgot your keys. Without keys to the building I could not get back in. I couldn't take the children out until he returned home from work. I never saw the mail. We rarely spoke to each other and he often visited bars after work. When he did talk he complained about how much money we were costing him so I tried my best to keep costs low and went without many of the basic items every woman needs.

When spring came I noticed the next door neighbor would take her daughter to the playground that was at the back of the building. She went around the same time every morning. One day I took a chance. I quickly got the children ready and brought them to the playground. When I noticed the lady packing up to go back in I gathered the children and made to go inside as well. I got to the door first and pretended to be looking for my keys. My plan worked; she became impatient waiting for me to find my keys. She said, "Oh, here I have mine right here". She let me in. This became our daily routine and after several weeks we became friends. When she asked me about the keys I simply said that he took them with him because they were on his key ring. As usual I was projecting a normal happy family.

One of the neighbors heard our commotion one evening and called the police. The same two officers came to our apartment. This time when the police came the law had changed and charges were automatically laid against my husband. They sneered at me when they said, "This time we don't need you to press charges, and we can press charges". They took my husband with them. I was terrified. They didn't understand. I had made my bed and had to lay in it. It would be worse for us if Kenny got in trouble. I knew Kenny would take it out on me.

It took several months for the case to land in court. I knew I could not leave the marriage and I wanted things to be as smooth as possible between us so in court I said that I could not remember the incident. It was mostly true. It was difficult to separate one incident from another. He was convicted anyway. Part of his punishment included attending anger management classes.

Anger management classes were not really successful. Every time he came home from class he was angry. After every class I could be sure of being hit. After the fourth class he called me his mother's name as he punched me. It was then that I realized it wasn't even me he was mad at.

Times were not all bad. He declared his great love for me and his children. He wrote songs. Hundreds of songs all proclaiming love for me. He could be very happy go lucky. Anyone would describe him as a nice guy. He was fun at a party. He had an infectious laugh. He was my husband and I loved him. I had heard his story. I had compassion for him because I identified with his wounds. They were the same wounds as mine. I understood hurt, rejection and self-hatred. I was sure he had been molested in childhood although he was not sure. He thought he may have memories from his birth family but he was not ready to confront them. He did his level best to bury them.

The counsellor from the anger management class asked me to come in and see him. He explained to me that Kenny had a sexual addiction. He explained that the affairs had nothing to do with me. He said it was obvious that Kenny loved me and his family. He said Kenny had a lot of guilt over the affairs that ended up coming out as anger. He wanted

Kenny to stay in counselling and for all of us to work together towards healing. I was willing to do that. Kenny had other plans. He finished the court ordered counselling and decided that he did not want to attend any more. Our life continued as usual.

I got a call at home one day. It was the manager of the local bank. The manager said he was sending the sheriff after me for failure to pay a credit card bill. He was going to confiscate my car. I told him that there must be a mistake. I did not bank at his bank, nor did I have a credit card from there. The manager proceeded to confirm my personal information. He had my name, address, birthdate, social insurance number, everything. I couldn't figure out how he had all of that personal information. I immediately walked with the two kids to the bank. I found out that my husband had forged my signature and had racked up a credit card balance of five thousand dollars. The bank manager wanted to have him charged with fraud. I asked for twenty-four hours to find out what was going on.

I confronted Kenny when he came from work and he immediately broke down. He sobbed like a child. He admitted to everything. I understood why I was not allowed to see the mail. The telephone bill alone had over nine hundred dollars charged to phone sex lines. There were three gas cards; several store cards and the bank visa. Every card was maxed out and the monthly payments had not been made.

One card was originally mine, in my name. It was a Sears's card with a two-hundred-dollar limit. Most of the girls acquired one while in university. We were told how to establish a good credit rating. Because I had good credit Kenny was able to show a paystub from his job at the Chrysler plant and increase the limit on the Sears card on the spot. He increased the limit to one thousand dollars. He spent the entire limit in one afternoon purchasing gifts for his latest mistress. She received jewelry, clothing, make up and trinkets. I was able to see a copy of the bill. This was how the whole thing had begun. After the first time with the Sears card it was easy to apply for and receive credit cards on the spot. At the final tally he had racked up bills totalling over twenty-five thousand dollars.

I had no idea how to get us out of this mess. Kenny sobbed and cried. He said he didn't understand himself and he was so sorry. He promised that everything was going to change from now on. No more anything. No more partying, no more women, no more spending, no more violence. He said I was the best thing that had ever happened to him and he knew that most women would not have stayed with him as I had done. He loved me and would do whatever I asked. He wanted me to keep him from being charged with fraud.

I consulted a financial advisor. In the end I assumed responsibility for the debt which kept him from being charged with fraud and together we claimed bankruptcy. The car was confiscated but we didn't lose anything else.

Things did change. I had the keys, I could come and go. I got the mail every day and took care of the bills. My basic needs were being met again. Kenny came home from work instead of going out to the bar. He never hit me again. He stopped seeing other women and started spending time with the family. He came to the playground at the back of the building and started taking the kids swimming. He even made breakfast a few times on the weekend. I was happy with the changes and hopeful for the future.

We enjoyed a solid year of happiness before he met a new friend. It started all over again. He started going out, started drinking again, started doing drugs, started staying out, started spending and started seeing other women. He left the house one day in February and didn't return for three weeks.

The children took it very hard when he was gone. I tried to make up answers to their questions as best I could. "Daddy's just at work, he has to work late". "Daddy was home but you were sleeping". It did not really work, they just wanted Daddy. It breaks your heart when your child is waiting at the window for hours and then goes to bed with tears wondering why Daddy did not come home.

This became our new cycle. He would leave every year in February. He would say he just didn't love me at all and he just could not be a father. He did not want to be a husband or a father.

He would party and cavort and stay wherever or with whichever woman he was currently seeing. He would come back in three, five or eight weeks, crying and saying İ don't know why I do this. I love you and the kids and I do want to be a husband and a father". I believed him when he said he did not love me and I believed him when he said he did. He was telling the truth each time. I was sure of that. I kept taking him back and we would be happy again until next February. Then the children would cry again. I always told them that Daddy loved them. They blamed me when Daddy went away.

Another day Kenny did not come home after work. I got a call the following day from the police. Kenny and a friend had been in a car accident. He was not hurt very badly but he was charged with driving while intoxicated, leaving the scene of an accident and evading the police. I needed to fetch him. When I arrived an officer filled me in on what had happened. There had been an actual chase from the police after they were caught soliciting women downtown. They made it across the border but speeding away from the border crossing, Kenny lost control of the vehicle and crashed it. There would be no evasion or solicitation charge from the other side of the border so he was lucky the officer said.

This was the beginning of the end for me. Eight years of this marriage had begun to wear me out. I could not stomach any more. Something about my husband soliciting prostitutes from the streets of downtown Detroit was the line in the sand. I knew there would never be intimacy with him again. It would not be safe. I knew the marriage was ending for me.

I told him that this was the last time I was going to take him back. I told him how much his departures hurt me and the children. I said if he did not change his behavior or if he ever left us again that I would be done. I would not take him back again. I tried my best to make sure that he understood that I was serious and meant what I said. He promised to change and promised that he would never leave again. I did not believe him.

I made plans to move the family to a cooperative housing subdivision. Rents were higher but if I was left alone again I would be able to get a subsidized rent atomically. As it was before when Kenny would disappear, I would be left with children to provide for and no money. I needed a way to protect and provide for us. I knew it was only a matter of time before he would leave us again. This housing option was a good opportunity for me to put some stable things into place.

Long before February came He and I had discussion after discussion after discussion. We both knew that he could not change his behavior and that he would leave again. He could not help himself. I needed him to understand that I was finished. I could not continue living this way. We agreed that when the time came we would separate. I promised to remain supportive as much as I could. I would assume full responsibility for the children. He would not have to bear the burden anymore. He was relieved. He told me that he understood.

Together we looked for an apartment for him. Together we furnished it. Together we prepared. He found a new female friend. He called me from work one night to say that he was not coming back. He said he would always love me and he thanked me for making the separation easy for him. We both cried. I said it was going to end up ok for all of us. He told me he would call me in a few days. I hung up the phone. I was one part relieved, one part afraid, one part exhausted, all parts heartbroken. I cried myself to sleep. It was over.

At around five am he was back pounding on the door begging me to let him in. He changed his mind, he didn't want to lose us. I peeked out the window. There was a woman waiting in a truck on the street in front of my house. I refused to open the door. Kenny begged and pounded on the door for over an hour and left only after I threatened to call the police. This is the only part the children heard and saw. Daddy was at the door wanting in and Mommy wouldn't let him in. They did not understand why.

The separation was hard on all of us. His weekend visits with the children would last about an hour and then he would call and say, "Come get your kids, I can't handle them". I would go and pick them up. The children did not understand, they cried incessantly for Daddy.

I had planned an afternoon at the local corn festival with the children. They were excited all morning waiting for the time when we would go. About thirty minutes before we were set to leave I received a call from a friend. "Don't take the kids to the corn fest", she said. "Kenny is there with another woman and he has her son on his shoulders, Noah does not need to see that". Once again I covered for him and told the children that I had changed my mind and we would not go to the festival. Once again the children were upset with me.

Back home in Eastern Canada my mother was dying. It was my father who had everyone worried. The stress of caring for my mother for the past six years had taken a toll on him. He was drinking heavily each evening and my aunts were concerned for his heart. I had asked Kenny to relocate to Eastern Canada. I thought the slower pace of life may do him some good. He was worried that he would not be able to feed his addiction. He especially enjoyed frequenting clubs that featured exotic dancers. There were none of those clubs in our small town. During the separation I asked him again to consider Eastern Canada. I told him about the concern for my father's health and how much dad could use my help. Kenny did not want to go. Kenny said I could go. Take the children and go. I'm not much of a father anyway. I'll visit when I can probably for March break he said. It will be better for all of us if you go.

I made plans to go, I arranged a moving truck and bought airline tickets. Two days before we were set to leave Kenny changed his mind. He said he didn't want us to go. I had to cancel everything. I lost my deposits. A week later he said we should go again. A week after that he changed his mind again and said we couldn't go. I stayed on this roller coaster for several months until the day of the corn festival. That was the day I decided that I was leaving Ontario and returning to Eastern Canada. It was summer 2004. This time I made arrangements quietly and only told Kenny the night before that we were leaving.

CHAPTER FOUR

Creating Invisibility

Babies and children hold a key in
the processing of grief

When we got to Eastern Canada, I had six months with my mother before she died.

I never knew my mother. I never had a full conversation with her, just a couple of sentences here and there. I always hated my mother. She was hard on me and nice to my brother. I felt she was hard on my father. She was not the right match for him. I wished he would divorce her. Whenever I had a problem with my mother and brought it to my father he would take her side. *You know she's wrong, She is my wife. I have to live with her.*

When I returned home to Eastern Canada there would not be any conversations either. My mother could not talk. She was diagnosed with two degenerative diseases, Shy Dragger Syndrome and Parkinson's. She was losing control of her body functions. She could barely swallow; she couldn't walk or take care of her own needs. My father was doing everything for her. He got her up at six every morning. He washed her, changed her diaper, dressed her, fed her and then got himself ready for work. Everyone called him a saint for the way he took care of her. He was dedicated and giving to a fault. While he was at work she was visited by two nurses each day. She had homemakers taking care of her needs.

The children and I moved in to the house across the street from my parents. I was able to visit every day before and after work. I helped out as much as I could. I could stay with Mom for a few hours in the evening so dad could get out and relax for a bit. Mom would insist that her most intimate needs were taken care of by Dad alone. It was humbling for me to help as well. My father had taken a piece of cardboard and printed the alphabet on it in large letters. When my mother had something to say she pointed to the letters on the board and spelled out her message. We figured out what she was saying. She could barely point but she made a good attempt. I teased her and told her that she must have Alzheimer's too because she could no longer spell. What was really happening was that the Parkinson's shake made it difficult for her to point to only one letter on the board. Instead of pointing to g-o she pointed to g-m. I told her she was losing her mind. It made us laugh.

When I saw my mother in the state she was in I truly came to love her. The woman I knew before was very proud. It was easy to embarrass her or make her angry. Now she had to be carried, cleaned and fed. In spite of all this she displayed such grace. That was the word I use to describe it. She had grace. She was no longer bitter as I remembered her. She would laugh at her own body functions. If you tried to stand her up invariably she would pass out and land on the floor. As she came to on the floor she would drool, *down again? Yes, mom, we're on the floor.* We would laugh. She was only ninety-two pounds but it was hard to get a ninety-two-pound woman up off the floor. Especially when as soon as you got her up she would pass out again.

It was not easy taking care of her. I had six months with her and I found it hard. My dad had six years. The six years were very stressful for him. When she drooled I would call her gross and we would laugh together. When she wanted me to shave her legs or clip her toe nails, I would say, "yuk!" I told her I was too young and immature to handle this stuff and she would laugh again.

She was very good at communicating through eye movements. Boy could she roll her eyes. You could tell her mood by the eye rolls. She still wanted things in the house the way she wanted them and she expected everyone to comply completely with her wishes. When she argued with my father she used her eyes. He took to turning his chair towards the wall. *I may as well talk to the wall as to talk to her.* She would sit in her chair roll her eyes and drool. *If you guys are going to argue I'm leaving the room.* Then everyone would laugh.

Family and friends visited daily and kept Mom up to date on all the latest gossip from town. We helped her play cards by holding them for her. She would indicate which card she wanted to play with eye movements. If the person holding her cards could not understand the eye movements she would try pointing a finger with the Parkinson's shake while her eyes gestured bigger and bigger. It was a funny sight to see.

We tracked her fluid intake and output for the doctor. The sheet would record so many ounces of this or that. We always put water on the sheet when she was really drinking whisky or beer. She could not inhale the cigarettes that I held to her mouth but she wanted them anyway. *Finish it* she would say after a couple of puffs. *It's gross, covered in drool. I'm not smoking that.* I stubbed them out. I told her she was wasteful and she would laugh again. The six months I spent with my parents were as lighthearted as I ever remember my family being. These days facing sickness and death were the best family days of my life. These days are so precious to me. I wondered what life might have been like.

I learned that Mom really did love me. She showed it in the ways that she could. I learned to be happy with that. We made our peace. She played the hand that God gave her. She was tough, a hard worker and to everyone else, she was a giver.

Finding out that she was a giver shocked me. I did not experience her as a giver but I believe the people who told me she was. When I thought back there was a time when she had given away all of the new school clothes and supplies I had bought for myself before leaving for camp. She had given my stuff to a cousin and when I asked her why she replied, "don't be selfish, you have more than she does." In retrospect my mother was a giving person.

I found out more about my mother's life at her wake and funeral then I ever knew before. People were generous at the wake to tell me stories about her. It was like I hadn't even met the person they were talking about. The person they described did not sound like the woman I knew. I wished I had known her as a woman and not just as my mother. It seemed I had a limited picture of who she was. I vowed then to make sure my children knew who I was as a person and as a woman not just as their mother. It was a great lesson. I remain thankful for that. I was twenty-seven when my Mom died in February 2005. Simultaneously I made one of the biggest mistakes of my life. One that I truly regret. I told my father that my brother had molested me.

At the time I didn't think about what my telling him would do to him. Hindsight is twenty/twenty vision. It was selfish of me to tell him at that time. He had way too much going on in his life. His plate was full. I just needed to get it out. I couldn't hold it in anymore. I didn't think of him. The news was devastating to him.

When my mom died, I lost both my parents. I lost my father to the bottle. He held up until after the funeral and disappeared after that. I didn't see him or speak much to him for months. I missed him. I missed the lighthearted nature of the previous six months, I felt so alone again. He gave me my mother's house. It had been our agreement; it was my inheritance. He gave it to me just as it was the day she died in it. I moved my family into the house. I had a hard time dealing with all of her things. The house itself held too many memories for me. I was struggling with grief.

My father came out of his fog when he met another woman. He had purchased another house for himself and moved her into the house. Less than one year following my Mom's death he remarried. After the wedding my father's new wife said to me that she was not comfortable with the housing arrangement. The new house was to be my brothers in the event of my father's death. She said that my brother would put her out of the house when my father died She would have nowhere to live. I decided to give my father back mom's house so that he could provide for the needs of his new wife.In March, my husband came to visit. He wanted me to take him back. He said he was ready to move to Eastern Canada. He had a woman in Ontario but he said she meant nothing to him. He wanted me to be intimate with him. I pointed out that he was asking me to participate in cheating on her. He had not changed; moving to Eastern Canada would not make any difference. He cut his visit short and went back to Ontario. The children were disappointed again and again, they blamed me for it. They just wanted Daddy.

My heart was broken open for my children. I pitied them. My son cried and cried for his father. He was not doing well. He hated school and was consumed by thoughts of Daddy. For months, every day he said to me, "I just want my dad".

The following winter I called my husband to discuss the issue. He told me he was stable and doing better. It was just before Christmas. I decided to send my son to his father. The plan was that he would finish the school year. I had a sense that it would not last that long. I thought my son might see who his father was, get to know him and be able to connect. I didn't want my son to be alone so I decided to send his sister with him. I put my children on an airplane to Ontario and immediately began to sink into despair without them.

My instinct in believing it would not last to end of the school year was correct. In February my husband died after colliding with a utility truck driving home from the night shift. He had fallen asleep at the wheel and veered into the other lane. One year and fifteen days after my mother died, my children and I lost Kenny forever. His twenty-two-year-old girlfriend died in the crash with him. We were twenty-eight years old. He died one week before my son's eighth birthday.

Kenny and I were not legally separated when he died; I was the legal spouse. The funeral arrangements were made by me. Having mistresses come to the wake was difficult. I could tell who they were by the way that they cried. I would have liked to throw them out of the funeral home but I did not. I would have liked to scream at them but I kept quiet as usual. I couldn't believe they would come to the wake. I understood that they needed to come. I was the wife; Kenny and I were very emotionally connected until the moment he died. I understood the mistresses felt emotionally connected as well.

One mistress had the audacity to put a photograph into the breast pocket of my husband's suit. I was so angry when I saw that. I experienced white hot fuming anger. Later when I was alone with him I took the photo out. I intended to destroy the photo. As I looked at the photo of this woman and her child I realized that it didn't matter anymore. She was not the first, nor was she the last. There would be no more mistresses. I put the photo back into his pocket and asked the staff to close the casket. Two years later when the financial affairs of the estate were being settled, one mistress sued me for money that Kenny owed her. She claimed to have been a common law spouse. The claim was false but she had forged rent receipts. In order to fight this woman in court I would have had to go back to Ontario and summon our friends as witnesses against her claims. I would have had to listen to her story. I would have had to refute it. I would have to delve into the pain from my marriage and talk about all of the affairs. I would have to show that she was one of many. I was physically very sick when this was happening. I lost a lung. I had no strength to fight. The lawyer I consulted advised me that this situation was not going to go away and that if I did not settle out of court, I would be summoned to court. I would have to appear at my own expense. He advised me that she would settle out of court for half of the estate. I suggested that I was married for nine years and that I had paid into our insurance policy, she had not. She had been dating him less than one year. I suggested perhaps she would accept one tenth of the estate. The lawyer laughed at my suggestion.

I was the one who had stabilized the financial affairs of my family. I was the one who had insisted on having an insurance policy. It was my way of trying to secure some stability for my family. I couldn't understand how anyone could challenge that stability. I felt violated again. I could not believe that God would do this to me. This was the repayment for being a faithful wife. I had been faithful physically and I had been faithful in honoring my husband. I did not deserve this.

I did not have the funds to travel to Ontario to challenge her claims. I did not want to delve into that pain and stir up painful emotions for me or my children. I settled out of court and one of my husband's many mistresses received half of the estate I had diligently worked to build. I lost seventy-five thousand dollars. After the settlement and because I did not challenge her claim, I also lost my survivor benefit through the Canada Pension Plan.

CHAPTER FIVE

Smashing into Stillness

In spring 2005 I had just started seeing a new boyfriend. I knew the mother of this guy. She told me about her son. He sounded wonderful and I could tell that she loved him very much. She said he needed and deserved a good woman like me. When he was home for a visit she would invite me over for coffee to meet him. He was living in Ontario but it was her desire that he would move back to Eastern Canada and she felt sure that he would do so soon.

The appointed day came and I went to his sister's home for coffee where his mother was babysitting. Ian was visiting his niece and nephew. The meeting was good but nothing exceptional. We had similar looks; he had wavy blonde hair, clear skin and blue eyes. Both sides were equally satisfied at the meeting. We had both been willing to meet the other based on his mother's suggestion. He finished his vacation and returned to Ontario. It was several months before he did move back home to Eastern Canada and we had the opportunity to go to dinner with some mutual friends.

I had cried so many nights over Kenny that it was nice to go out and have some fun. I asked aloud in my car one day if I could ever stop crying over him. Then along came this good looking guy who says let's go have some fun and here, smoke this. It was pot. Ian was fun. I had fun when I was with him. He had a plan for fun every weekend. There was a dance somewhere or a party being held. Or we just went to the bar. We played cards with friends or just hung out. He took me hunting and fishing and four wheeling. It wasn't long before I was in love and he moved in. Smoking marijuana did help slow my thoughts but I did not really like it. I felt like I was doing something wrong and I was paranoid when I smoked it. I wanted to fit in so when it was around especially if we were with a group of people I smoked some. Sometimes it felt carefree to escape my life for a bit.

Ian too had a difficult childhood and once again I identified with his wounds. Before I met him he had been manipulated, bribed and used. He had been betrayed like I was. He had been robbed of his family. He felt used and rejected. I understood how he felt.

After my husband died, Ian asked me to become the mother of his child. I was very humbled by his request. He had tears in his eyes as he told me what a good mother I was and how we could become a family. What a request. I did want another child and knowing that he was estranged from his other children I agreed thinking that being a father would be good for him.

I became pregnant and was looking forward to the future. Less than three months later the relationship ended. It did not end well. I'm still not sure what went so terribly wrong. Perhaps Ian was fearful after I got pregnant. Maybe he was not ready to be responsible for a family. Ian returned to doing hard drugs and started sleeping around. I was unaware that Ian had had a previous problem with cocaine but when I found out it really frightened me. I did not want to go down that road. I tried to have an intervention for him. It was long before the show that now plays on television but it was the same idea. In attendance were the counsellor, his mother, my father and me. He did come into the room but someone had told him about the intervention plan just before the appointment and he was very angry. His response was immediate. He exploded and left. He forbade his mother having anything to do with me or the baby. The relationship was over.

When the relationship fell apart, Ian and I both fell apart. He began following me wherever I went. He would show up at the house and make threats. He tried to run me off the road several times, even when I had the children in the car. I could not believe what was happening. I was pregnant. When I was not home he would go to the house and threaten the children and the babysitter. He threatened friends of mine. He threatened both of our families. He forbade his family to have anything to do with me or the baby. He thought I was out to steal his friends and he wanted to destroy my reputation. *When I get through talking about you, you won't be able to lift your head in this town.* It was a pronouncement of shame on me. One day a family member of his called me to tell me he was on his way to see me and that he had a gun. He was threatening to shoot me. I fled with the children and landed in a woman's shelter. In the end a peace bond was put on him and he was convicted of criminal harassment.

It was very stressful. I was vomiting profusely daily. My nerves were shot; I would shake uncontrollably. I was concerned for the baby. I had a hard time calming myself. I was so confused. I thought we were in love and were building a family together. I didn't know who this guy was. This was not the same guy who just three short months ago asked me to become the mother of his child. I was heartbroken again. I was shattered. I was gutted. I literally felt like my heart had been ripped out of my chest. I had physical chest pain. I cried myself to sleep every night.

When it was safe to leave the shelter we came home. I had ordered a mobile home where we had been planning to build our family. It was ready for set up. I purposed myself to make a nice, peaceful environment for my family. Ian's threats did the trick. People everywhere distanced themselves from the situation and from me. Nobody would babysit for me anymore. I had to withdraw from evening Lamaze class. I did not want to fuel the situation in any way so I stayed away from anyone who was his friend. My father and his new wife were disgusted by the whole thing and they kept their distance as well. There was no need to pronounce shame on me; I had plenty of shame. And embarrassment, I had plenty of that as well. I felt totally unlovable, worthless and stupid. I was a fool to think that anyone could ever love me. Now I saw how stupid it was to agree to become pregnant without being married. *what was I thinking?* I wasn't thinking. I had been swept away by some foolish desires confusing them with love. The script in my head went, *stupid, stupid girl. You deserve everything that you got. You do not deserve to be a mother. Look at what you have put your children through. You will never be loved and you will never love you stupid, filthy* _____.

I hired a few guys to help with the yard. I got the kids a dog and hired someone to build a dog house for him. The mini home was good. It was in a nice spot. One of the men I hired to help with the yard was sick and could not come one day so he sent his brother as a replacement.

That's how I met my second husband. He came to work on the yard in place of his brother. He was infatuated with me instantly. He said

I should date him. I was not interested in dating and I was pregnant with another man's baby. My second husband didn't believe that I was pregnant. He didn't know how heartbroken I was and that I was crying myself to sleep every night. I was good at wearing the happy face during the day and whenever I had to care for the kids but at night when I was alone I cried rivers of tears. My second husband was persistent in his asking. He even made a pronouncement that I would marry him someday. I thought he was nuts. Bold and nuts! I was never getting married again.

He told me his story. It's the same story again. It's a story of abuse and violence. It's a story of pain, fear, loss and rejection. It's a story of survival. His response was hurt, fear and anger. When you hear a story like this, compassion rises in your heart and you understand the response. When I heard my second husband's story I was proud of his ability to survive all that he had been through and I saw that he was a good man. He couldn't do enough to help me. Whatever I needed I had only to ask and he would be there. He kept asking me to go out and I kept saying no. He would tell me that I would change my mind someday. I would laugh at that. It was comforting to feel that there was someone I could call if I needed help. There was something endearing about my second husband. He was full of crap and honest at the same time. He was not educated beyond grade eight but some of the things he said were insightful and full of simple wisdom.

He didn't believe that I was pregnant until I agreed to dance with him at his birthday party in December. It was my birthday too. Originally I said no I would not come but decided to surprise him at the last minute. He was happy I was there and it turned out well because some of his buddies ended up needing a sober drive home. I was sober. While dancing he noticed the pregnant belly. I thought it meant that he would stop asking me out. Stop pronouncing that I would marry him someday. He was not at all comfortable with children. He avoided children at all costs. He was terrified of babies and could not handle when a child cried. He was so scared he said not to call him if I needed a drive to the hospital when I was in labor. I could call for anything else but not that. He was worried that the birth could occur in the car. I thought it was funny and promised that I would not call him for a drive. I promised not to give birth in his car.

My beautiful daughter was born at the end of January. I was still crying myself to sleep every night. I was still heartbroken that Ian did not love me. She looked so much like him. I was heartbroken that my daughter was born fatherless. I was heartbroken that I had three fatherless children. I could not provide for them the thing that they needed and desired the most. I felt that I was not enough for them and that it was my fault that they were fatherless. Nevertheless, it was my duty to be as good a mother as I could be so I did my best to be thankful for having them, hopeful about the future and to show them only my happy face.

Noah and Nicole were enthralled with their new baby sister. Noah was the sweetest and gentlest boy as he held his baby sister. He counted all of her fingers and toes to make sure she had the right number. He smiled at her and whispered in her ear how cute she was and how much he loved her. Nicole's eyes glistened with tears as she held her baby sister. She couldn't believe how small and beautiful her sister was. Nicole was very happy to have a sister instead of a brother. Noah was less thrilled at that. It was a good thing that Danielle was so small and beautiful or he may not have liked her at all. Nicole was very helpful to me and was the best big sister ever. She wanted to watch and help with everything. When the nurse came to weigh and measure their sister, both children watched every step. They insisted on hearing her heartbeat too when the nurse took out the stethoscope. They wanted to make sure everything was alright. It was- she was a healthy baby.

Babies and children hold a key in the processing of grief. Our new life began. I decided to stop crying and life was peaceful, quiet and calm.

A few weeks after the baby was born I decided to take a break for a couple of hours and I went ice fishing. To make a long story short the jeep we were travelling in slid off the road as we were leaving. The jeep slid close to seventy-five feet down the side of an embankment and was stopped from crashing at the bottom only by a clump of trees. I had been sitting in the front passenger seat with no seatbelt and no footwear. My feet had gotten wet during the fishing. They were frozen so I was warming them on the dashboard. It was frightening during the decent. We tried to brace ourselves. Hitting the bottom could kill us. Because my feet were on the dashboard and I was not wearing a seatbelt, when we hit the clump of trees I was slammed up against the upper right hand corner of the windshield. My head didn't go through the windshield because I bent it forward. My right side took the brunt of the impact as I was slammed up against the corner of the windshield.

When the vehicle stopped we were perched precariously on top of the tree trunks and branches that we had plowed over before hitting the clump that stopped us. Movement caused the vehicle to tilt and it was tricky getting out. We did get out but I was shoeless. Someone was brave enough to go back in after some footwear for me. We then had to climb up the side of the embankment and walk about a mile to the nearest house to borrow a phone. We called for a ride. I knew I was not exactly right. I wasn't really hurt. I thought I must be in shock. I was breathing ok but I just didn't feel right.

What I didn't know at the time was that bacteria had been growing in my right lung. My guess is that the impact created a hole in the diseased lung tissue and my lung collapsed. I developed symptoms that mimicked the flu. In the next two weeks I went to the doctor and the emergency room and was told to rest at home and drink plenty of fluids. By the end of two weeks I was so weak I could barely stand. I knew something was wrong. I was seen by a doctor and sent to the emergency room immediately. The lung issue was discovered and I was sent to the city for emergency surgery.

It was supposed to be a simple laser exploration to figure out what was going on. When you sign the consent form for surgery you don't really pay attention to the risks. This or that may possibly happen. When I woke up the nursing staff told me I was lucky to be alive. I was unable to breathe on my own and was hooked up to a respirator. An emergency thoracotomy had been performed. It's a surgery to remove a lung. Most of the patients who have this type of surgery have cancer and a shorter life expectancy. Apparently after the surgeon opened the side of my chest cavity he tried to take a sample of the diseased tissue. When he touched the scalpel to the tissue, the entire mass disintegrated and the diseased tissue fell into my chest cavity. It was very difficult to get the diseased tissue out. Three times on the table they thought I was a goner as they could not get me breathing.

Over and over I heard the same thing from hospital staff. *You are so lucky to be alive; you don't know how close you came to death.* Some even said, *You should be dead, I can't believe you are alive.* Staff that were present during surgery came to see me. Staff from other parts of the hospital came to see me because they heard about the new mother who almost died. They all said the same thing. I was lucky.

The bacteria ended up being from pigeons. Nobody could tell me how the bacteria got into my lung. I went into the hospital at the beginning of February and when I got out it was the end of April. The first time the nurses got me out of the bed I was to stand up for as many seconds as I could. It took four staff to help manage the equipment I was hooked up to. I was connected to oxygen, an epidural, two chest tubes, a catheter, and an intravenous fluid bag. Days later walking a few steps took enormous effort and four people with me just to make it to the chair beside the bed. Walking down the hall the next week was like a parade.

Slowly day by day I gained some strength. I was determined to get home as quickly as I could. I did everything the doctors told me to do. I walked when they told me and rested when they told me. I breathed into the machine as hard as I could when they told me to. I took the medication when they told me and trusted everything they said. Pieces of equipment came off me one by one. The epidural was the first to go. When that went I wanted it back. Pain medication taken by mouth was not nearly as effective as the epidural. That's when I knew I was really hurt. Just breathing was extremely painful. I knew then that this was no cake walk and that the comments of the hospital staff were true.

I had been paying a hefty weekly price for people to care for my children at home. I had to send the baby to a friend's mother who was being paid to care for her needs. While I was in the hospital in the city my father sent my cousin to visit me to make sure that I was going to live. If not for that I would have had no visitors outside of the hospital staff. I spent my days walking a few steps at a time trying to gain some strength and allowing my right side and chest to heal.

When I did get home I was nearly out of money, clearly not able to go to work and the only family I had outside of my children, my father, was barely speaking to me. *If it wasn't for bad luck I would have no luck at all.* I could walk but only a few meters at a time. I could barely lift my right arm. Washing my own hair was a problem. Opening doors was a problem. I was too weak to hold my own baby. I would sit in a rocking chair while someone handed me my baby. I could only hold her for a few minutes at a time.

It was time for the happy face again. The children had been very scared that mommy was going to die. They had just lost their father and the thought of losing me was unbearable and very frightening for them. I reassured them as best as I could that I was not going to die.

I did the best I could to gain enough strength to bring my baby home. My second husband was my diamond in the rough during this time. He became my knight in shining armor. He really came through for me. He drove me wherever I needed to go. Whatever I needed done, he did for me. He got my groceries, carried them in the house and helped me put them away. He came to see me every day. He encouraged me to play crib with him. He offered to help me wash my hair. He became less and less scared of the baby. One day I asked him to hold her for a minute while I did something else. It was the first time he held a baby in over twenty years. It became a daily habit for him to hold her. Each time he held her for a longer period.

As days turned into weeks and then months, I was able to watch as this man who had a hard and crusty exterior fell in love with an eight-pound beautiful blonde baby girl. Her blue eyes melted him. He loved to watch me with her. I had a particularly hard time trying to bathe her. I had to get into the tub and have one of the kids hand her to me. I could not lean over the side of the tub to wash her. When the baby was ready to come out of the tub, one of the kids had to take her until I got out. I dried off and robed so I could finish with her from there.

One of my favorite rituals with my children is massage time after the evening bath. I always sent my second husband home when it was bath time. One evening he asked to watch the ritual. I allowed him to stay and watch. He watched as I sang and cooed to her while drying her off and massaging baby lotion into her delicate skin. My second husband said he was really touched by the way I cared for my children. He watched me do many things for my children and he had helped me with a few things. He said he had never seen anyone get so excited to prepare a gift for their child. He said they were lucky to have the kind of home that I created for them. He knew that I tried to always put their needs and wants first. His mother had not shown that to him. He said his life would have been different if he had a mother like me. He was still asking me to marry him and proclaiming that someday I would.

I considered his request more seriously. He was a good man. He was loyal. *Maybe that's what I need, someone who will be loyal to me.* I thought that maybe I could be a good and loyal wife to him. By marrying him I could repay some of the kindness he had shown to me in my time of distress. *It could be a good marriage. It could be a quiet, simple marriage.* No other offers were going to come along. *Who would want a disabled single mother of three children.* I said I would marry him.

As we prepared for the wedding the next big thing happened.

CHAPTER SIX

Finding the Beginning

I knew he wouldn't let me die-he
wanted me to suffer and suffer
I was

knew I was adopted. It was no secret. Shortly after becoming civilians in 1980 I went with a friend who got a haircut at the neighbor's house. While my friend was in the chair having her hair cut the hair dresser started asking me the usual questions. *Who's your father? I was adopted.* After the cut was done, *I know exactly who you are. I know your birth mother. You are too good for her. You should never meet her.* She asked me not to tell my parents what she said. I agreed. Who would I tell? My mom made it perfectly clear that she alone was my mother and no one else. I didn't say a word when I got home. I was angry. I thought it was a terrible thing to say. I always wondered why my own mother did not want me but to say that I was too good for her was ridiculous. One couldn't be too good for her own mother.

Later that evening that same lady showed up at my house with a police officer. I answered the door. She asked to speak with my parents. I had a sinking feeling in the pit of my stomach. I knew I was going to be in trouble. What could I do, I had to get my parents. I went and hid in my room. To this day I have no idea what was said. After the lady left my mother came to my room and stuck her head in. *Never speak to that woman again.* I didn't. Soon the lady and her family moved away.

Years later after my mom died I saw the lady in the mall. She worked in the jewelry shop. As dad and I walked by I asked him, *is that that lady? Yes* he said. That was all. In my heart I said, someday I'm going to be brave enough to talk to her. I was not quite brave enough.

In the fall of 1997 as I prepared for my second wedding I received a phone call at home. It was adoption services calling *You have a sister and she has written you a letter. Would you like to receive it?* The sister had actually been looking for me for many years. The law did not allow siblings to look for each other so the process was stunted. My sister had been waiting years for the law to change and now it had. Would I like to receive the letter? I said yes. I hung up the phone. *Get in the car, we're going to the mall. I'm going to find that woman and talk to her.*

When we arrived at the mall she was not at work. I told my second husband I was going to get a coffee. I intended to sit on the bench outside the store until she came. I was not leaving without speaking to her. I went to A&W to get the coffee. That lady was in front of me in line. She turned around and saw me. *How are you? are you doing some shopping today? No, I came to see you. I knew some day you would.* She had twenty minutes before her shift started. She invited me to sit with her.

The day I was in her basement with my friend for the haircut, my sister and niece were upstairs in the kitchen. That lady's name is Edna. Her husband was the police officer that came with her to my house that evening. After she told her husband what she had said to me that afternoon he insisted that she come and tell my parents what had transpired.

Edna had wanted to adopt my niece. My sister had the baby too young and she could not look after her. While the adoption application was being handled my birth mother somehow interfered in the process. My birth mother had formerly been Edna's friend but there was bad blood after the adoption was thwarted. Edna was able to tell me about my mother, my sister, my brother and three other half siblings. It was a lot to take in. My birth mother was a troubled lady. Perhaps it was alcoholism or perhaps mental illness but probably it was a combination of the two. My birth mother was the town drunk. Her life was never pretty; it was full of drama.

I am one of her illegitimate children. She has three by my birth father. He was a business owner and she was his mistress. He was married when she met him but he said he was getting divorced. By the time his divorce came through they had been together for several years and my birth mother was pregnant. He did propose to her but she refused. She found out he had another woman pregnant at the same. She suggested he marry her. He did. I've been told that he spent the last part of his wedding night with my mother. I was born eight years later. They had a son between my sister and I.

My head was reeling. This was a roller coaster of emotion. I had to know more. In hindsight I should have slowed down and allowed adoption services to follow their process with me. The process is there for a good reason. They would have blotted out any identifying information in my sister's letter and allowed some things to sink in before moving the process along. As it was I went home and immediately telephoned my sister. She was in Alberta.

When she answered I said, *Is this Natalie? Yes. Hi, I hear you are looking for me, my name is Victoria.* She screamed and dropped the phone. *Oh my God, oh my God, oh my God, is that really you? My sister? My baby doll? Victoria, is that really you? Oh my God, oh my God, Oh my God.* It's a little much to get a phone call like that. I realize now. Now we roar laughing about it but at the time it was very intense. We stayed on the phone for about four hours. It was very difficult to think about hanging up. While it's hard to get to know someone over the phone we immediately had a connection. We had many things in common besides our DNA. For the next three days we were on the phone most of our waking hours. Finally, she said she could fly to see me for less than the cost of the phone bill. She made arrangements to fly down. She would land in the city and would stay with our brother. I had a full brother. Donald.

I was nervous during the drive to the city. It was intensely emotional. I had a brother and a sister. *Wow.* He was awesome. She was exactly what I expected. There was no mistake and no need for DNA testing to prove anything. My son looked exactly like my brother and so did I. My sister and I were very similar and nobody could tell our voices apart. It was an interesting study in nature versus nurture. She and I had the same mannerisms. We talked with the same cadence, we sat the same and gestured the same. All three of us have the same hair and eye color. It is mind blowing to be thirty years old and meeting your siblings for the first time. I sat there looking at them thinking *wow.* I was not just looking at them; I was studying them. Like looking at something you have never seen before, trying to figure out what it is. The only word my brain could formulate was, *wow.* Then somebody thinks they should say something or do something but everything you say sounds so stupid, *so, how are you?* Who are you is the question you want to ask. You know the answer will be complicated. So you stick with small stuff, *what do you do for a living? Nice house, how long have you lived here?*

We decided we would spend the weekend doing stuff we missed in childhood. We would go for a swim, drive go carts, go bowling, drive bumper boats and do any kid stuff we could think of. Each of us would do the activities the other suggested even if we didn't like doing it. My brother and I would play twenty questions but with only five questions. *Five questions! I need twenty questions to get to know my brother.* My brother is intensely private and would only answer five. Five questions and a weekend full of childhood activities. We would start in the morning. That was good. I needed time to figure out which five questions I would ask. I realize now that it was a protective measure on his part. His childhood was very difficult and he did not want to delve too far into it. At the time I was trying to figure out how to frame the five questions so that I could get the best and the most information out of him. I wanted to know who he was and how he felt about things. I wanted to know what made him happy and what made him sad. I wanted to know what he thought about everything. I wanted to see into his heart.

He was the most beautiful man I had ever seen in my life and I loved him instantly.

The weekend was a blast. I was ecstatic. I couldn't believe that I had a real brother. I was so happy to have a sister but to have a brother-that was something else entirely. I had a real brother that was normal. It was awesome. We swam and tried to drown each other. He did brotherly things like pulled my hair and tried to be better than me at everything we did. He tried to be smarter. He won go-carts but I won swimming. I found him brilliant and complex. He is kind hearted and sensitive. He has a decent sense of humor and he laughs easily. I did not want the weekend to end. It was very healing. On Sunday we were going to meet one last time before the weekend was over and it was time to go home. While there I was wondering what the relationship would look like from this point forward.

That was when my bubble burst. Donald told me that he was not interested in pursuing a relationship beyond the weekend. It was over for him. He was done. He had a family and did not want me to be a part of his life.

I was shocked. I tried not to cry in front of him. I tried to stay calm and I tried to stay polite until I got out of his house. I couldn't get out of his house fast enough. I couldn't believe what I heard. I felt totally manipulated and deceived. If he had told me on Friday what his intentions were I wouldn't have given my heart so easily and fully. I would have guarded my heart. I was crushed and rejected again. *Again!* I was so hurt.

I can understand. If my mom was not dead, I would never have met them. If my mom was alive I would have told adoption services to keep my sister's letter. Loyalty to the adopted family is drilled in over and over. Understanding does not ease the pain of rejection. I have a brother, he's mine but he's not. I can't have him. *There is nothing fair or kind about this life. Or this history of mine.* I think I cried all the way from the city back to a small town.

But boy was I mad! *What a jerk! No frigging fair! It's a good thing that he didn't tell me earlier because I'd have tried to drown him for real.* No matter how mad I am at him I can't help myself but to carry love for him in my heart.

Back home it was time to start some treatments to help the recovery from the surgery. I still had very significant pain and my progress was very slow. I was not better yet. I had expected to be fully recovered by this time. I was gaining weight due to lack of activity and I was still nursing my sore side as I now referred to it. Physiotherapy was a painful process. I was able to walk for seven minutes on the treadmill. Seven minutes seemed not much for a former athlete. On the slowest speed too., The turtle speed I called it. I had been on several different medications to help with the pain but I was not happy with these. I did not like how they made my brain feel.

When February came and there was no change in my pain level and no change in my restricted movement I was told it was now considered to be chronic. I had damage to the nerves in my side. I would never get better. There would be no end to the daily suffering I had been enduring. I would never work again and the atrophy in my side would not improve. There was a significant amount of scar tissue that would always be there as nothing could be done to remove it. For pain a suggested course of treatment was the introduction of cortisone injections into the nerves that run underneath the ribs. It would be a risky procedure and there were not many physicians in the province that would be willing to try but we could search someone out. There were pain management specialists in the city at the pain management center. The wait list for the center was three years. The good news was that there was a program. I was registered and on the wait list.

This news was devastating. I was furious to think that my condition was permanent. It was very frustrating. I had just turned thirty. I could live another fifty years. I did not want to live fifty years in pain. I did not want to live fifty minutes in pain. I wanted the pain to stop. I wanted my strength back. I wanted my agility back. I wanted my life back! *If I have to live fifty years in pain the surgeon should have let me die.* What use was saving a life if the life was to be lived in suffering and misery!

Bitterness took root in my heart instantly. There was a small hope that the shots could help with the pain. I needed to focus on that and focus on the upcoming wedding. We finally located an anesthetist that was willing to try giving the shots. His idea was to give two to six shots every six weeks. If cortisone did not work to deaden the pain he was willing to go one step further and try pure alcohol injections. Same treatment cycle. We would try the cortisone first.

We decided to relocate our family in order to be close to the anesthetist and closer to the pain management center. The injections were brutally painful. The needle first had to poke the rib itself and then be drawn back a bit in order to push ahead and find the nerve running underneath. I received six injections at each session. The first sessions were two weeks apart. It took two weeks to recover from the shots. After the shots it was very difficult to move. Breathing was painful much less walking. Any movement that required lifting my right arm, washing my face, brushing my teeth, opening doors, getting up and down stairs was excruciating. Life was agony every day.

After four sessions with the cortisone it was apparent that cortisone was not working at all. We progressed to alcohol injections. The thinking behind the pure alcohol was that it would deaden the nerve or kill the nerve permanently. I can tell you that alcohol injections make cortisone injections seem like a bee sting. This was where my mental strategies came in very useful. I would be somewhere else in my mind while the shots were being given. I made no sound. The doctor was not comfortable with my silence. *You need to make some sound when I contact the rib so I know I'm in the right spot. I might scream instead of just make a sound.* I have to laugh now, I can't remember if I screamed or cried, I just remember after the shot he said, "Ok, we can go back to silence". I was relieved. It was easier to take the shots when I could be somewhere else in my mind. Dissociating was very helpful in this case. With the alcohol I experienced success in one particular spot. The most painful spot was not affected by the alcohol so we thought to try phenol injections. It had never been done in Eastern Canada before.

The first injection of phenol made me pass out on the spot. When I came to the doctor did not want to continue. I begged him to complete the session. He agreed to proceed. I was really trying to use my mental strategy but I could not. I have never heard a scream like I screamed inside my head. I could not believe how much it hurt. It really burned. One of the injections missed the nerve and phenol burned inside my chest for two solid weeks. It recessed for two more weeks until it was absorbed by the body. You could visibly see the red burns come through my skin as the phenol travelled from the injection site at the top rib to the bottom rib. I watched as it travelled upwards in the same manner before disappearing.

After the second set of phenol injections neither the doctor nor I was interested in continuing. This avenue was exhausted. There would be no cure from the injections. My hope was gone.

I was drained of all energy. I had no physical, mental or emotional energy left. As hope left me despair came. My will to live left me and I began to despise the doctor who had saved my life.

After several days' tears did come. Along with grief. Overwhelming grief for what I now had to endure-living. Tears slid down my face every morning when I woke up. I prayed before I went to sleep every night that I would die in my sleep.

During my waking hours I felt like I was hanging on to sanity by the fingernails. I could easily choose to slip away at any moment. The pain was so severe and so constant that it overtook my thoughts and focus. I could not easily concentrate on anything else. Movement caused excruciating agony. I did not want to move at all so I stayed as still as possible and willed myself to die.

Even though my second husband encouraged me to live our marriage was already in trouble. Something had changed right after the wedding. I found myself again in an unhealthy relationship. As my second husband was trying to convince me that my family needed me I could not think of them. Taking care of them was too much for me. They would all have to do without me I just couldn't bear my life anymore. It was all too much. Too much pain, physically and emotionally. *Too much, too much, too much.* There was no purpose to my life. I had accomplished nothing, I was no good to anybody and nobody had ever wanted me. I did not know why I had been born in the first place. I failed at everything and made colossal mistakes. There was no way to go back. *The world would have been a better place if I had not been in it.* Some people may have called this thought process depression but I did not see it as that. I saw it as just plain facing the facts. I was no good. No good at all.

God had seen fit to punish me over and over and when he was through he was going to send me to hell. All because I hated him when I was three. Or maybe because of all the sins I had committed since; sexual immorality, murder (if you think it you have done it), drugs, stealing, lying, dishonoring parents, I had done it all.

I was so angry with God. *How could he punish me so much? Why did I deserve so much punishment? What chance did I have of ever being good?* I tried to be good for as long as I could but the standard was set too high. I couldn't achieve it.

I knew he wouldn't let me die-he wanted me to suffer and suffer I was.

CHAPTER SEVEN

Colliding with Life

I was pissed off at God

This is the state I was in when I was invited to attend church in 1998.

My relationship with God was one of contempt, disbelief, shame. Feelings of being punished, condemned and destined to suffer forever.

I had never doubted the existence of God, never failed to address him by that name. I thought I was inadequate despite my efforts at being good, being perfect, being acceptable.

I was pissed off at God.

There is this place in me; call it what you like. It's a place where my thoughts intersect with the intentions of my heart. I know that whatever the thought or decision is, it is right. A place where I am at peace with myself. I know I have to do whatever that place dictates or I shall never rest, a place I acknowledge as being God in me. It sounds like a funny thing to say but I have no other way to describe it. People may choose to call it conscience but it is something different than when my conscience is bothering me. It's just a knowing...knowing that whatever it is...it is the right thing, the right place, the right decision, the right direction. It is truth, peace and rest. I know that I know. I call it God.

I had not been in that place or experienced that anomaly for a very long time. I wasn't expecting to find God by going to church. I agreed to go to church to get the person off my back. The one who was insistently asking me to go.

As I walked into the church I thought, *this is not a church. This is a warehouse building in an industrial park. There are no stained glass windows, there's no altar, and there aren't even any pews. What kind of a church is this?* There was a rock band at the front. Stacking chairs in rows for people to sit on. The music was not bad, I actually kind of liked it. *The people here are weird* Everyone was raising their arms above their heads waving to the ceiling. I figured this was a cult. I was not comfortable.

I did notice the diversity of the people. Some were black, some white, some young, and some old. Some of the people were dressed in church clothes, some in jeans and some in biker gear. They were all waving their arms. One lady started running all around the perimeter of the room waving her arms. *Oh my. What is this? This has to be a cult.* I was not comfortable. Not in the least. *What am I doing here? This is the last time I will ever be here. I can't wait to get out of here.*

There was no priest at this church. A guy in a suit came to the microphone. I can't tell you what he started talking about; I wasn't really listening. I can't remember. This is the part I do remember. At one point he became frustrated. He flung off his suit jacket, waved it in the air and said, "I can't preach this today because I am so sick and tired of what people are saying about the Swiss Air crash! Everywhere I go, people say, "Well, it was God's will that they should go. It was their time to go or God needed more angels in heaven". *God does not need more angels in heaven!* The Pastor flung his suit jacket over the back of one of the stacking chairs. He shouted into the air, *It is not God's will that people die! God does not pluck airplanes out of the sky and fling them into the ocean killing 229 people! Satan does that! I'm tired of people blaming God for the things that Satan does.*

The pastor went on to talk about how the devil is real. He explained how we do not really believe that the devil is real. He outlined the destruction in the lives of people and the wickedness abounding on this planet all due, he explained, not to God but to the enemy of God. *Satan is a being as alive as you and me causing wickedness, sickness, destruction and death.* He pointed to rebellious youth, drugs, alcoholism, lewdness, sexual perversion, violence, disease, murder and death. He called all of these things evil and placed the responsibility for all of these things on Satan who he said had a lease on the world we live in.

I knew it was true of me, I said those exact words about the victims of the air disaster., *It was their time to go.* I blamed God for everything. I had heard of the devil but I did not believe that the devil was real.

The pastor explained that God was a God of love and that the world He created had no perversion. He was not the author of death but the author of life. He pointed to Jesus who said that we would know the truth and the truth would set us free. Jesus who said I am the way the truth and the life. He told us the story of Jesus who could have condemned a woman caught in the act of adultery. The punishment for her in that time was stoning to death. Jesus said to the men, who would have carried out the sentence, let he who has no sin cast the first stone.

Jesus, the pastor said was the only person qualified to stone the woman to death and yet he chose not to. *It is not God's will that any should die in sin which is why He offers us forgiveness and eternal life. God is a God of mercy. God is faithful to forgive our sin when we ask Him to.*

Now I was re-thinking my position. *Could it be true? Could the devil be real? Is God real? If God is real, who is He? What's he really like?* At the end of the service the Pastor invited us to accept Jesus into our hearts. He said we should ask Jesus to forgive our sins and be the Lord of our life. I figured there could be no harm in asking. I asked Jesus to forgive me and to become the Lord of my life.

CHAPTER EIGHT

Speaking the Truth

I gave a statement about my abuse
to the police.

The years between that fateful day in 1998 and another fateful day in 2013 I will fill in as we go.

In 2013 after a long battle in my own mind and heart I gave a statement about my abuse to the police. The other girls I suspected had been abused by my brother had begun to invade my thoughts and dreams once again. I felt responsible or wondered if I bore any responsibility in their fates. Certainly as a child I bore none but did I bear any now; this many years later that was the question. *Why are these thoughts invading my being now?* Invading is the only appropriate word as I was unable to ignore the thoughts or to keep them contained. With as much experience as I had compartmentalizing my thoughts, I found myself beginning to lose control over when thoughts came to me, how long they stayed and what reactions they produced.

The very fact that I was once again experiencing invading thoughts proved to me that I did bear some responsibility. I bore responsibility to my own moral code. The code in me that allows me to live peaceably with myself. The code that says, *do the right thing. Tell the police.* I didn't think telling the police was an option. I thought there was a statute of limitations. Since I didn't tell all those years ago I couldn't tell now.

I have great difficulty asking for anything. It comes from childhood trauma. Neglect, the culprit there. Being forced to beg for something hideously cruel. Asking implies being needy in some way. Showing vulnerability. Things I avoid doing. I felt lead to ask Len, the husband of a friend. He listened and told me a story of his own. He answered my inquiry with a question, "could you live with it if he did it again tonight?"

It was a direct piercing question. The answer came immediately with equal piercing clarity. *No.* I left the discussion knowing that first thing in the morning I would go and tell my story to the police.

Sexual assault cases are difficult to prove and historical cases 30 years old are trickier. I gave my statement with no expectations about the outcome. I hoped that somebody could prove to me what was true and what wasn't. I gave my statement hoping to validate the other victims. To relieve myself of the responsibility of thinking that someone else had been hurt as I had been and I did nothing to help. I needed the police to share the responsibility just in case. It was a huge decision. I had to consider the consequences of coming forward. I'm glad I took the time to think about it. I made sure I had a support system in place. I had to manage my expectations.

I was under the false delusion that I was in control. I had developed coping skills. I faltered in my belief that it was actually true.

This gnawing pull to tell raged against the sense that what happened was too long ago and too insignificant to matter to anyone.

My credibility was in question. My credibility with myself. I could hardly believe what happened to me, *how could I expect anybody else to believe me?* Either way I had to know that I did everything I could to help any other possible victims no matter how late. *Better late than never as they say.*

While giving that statement I found thoughts racing in and out of my awareness while my lips were speaking a few miles back. *Tell this, tell that.* Words seemed to ball up and lodge in my throat. I could not get past them.

I felt repeatedly nauseous. I needed to soothe myself. I was trying to mask just how much distress I was in. I felt shocked at my own inability to maintain control. The vile words were in my ears the entire time. Taunting me over and over, *nobody will believe you, you like being raped, if you ever tell, I'll kill you; bitch!*

I felt very childlike. The shame of my youth cloaked me like a thick, heavy blanket. I wondered if I was visibly shaking. *At least I would know the truth.* I tried to employ all of my coping mechanisms during the statement. I asked for a washroom break. I felt sick. It was the first time I said those things out loud. I was dry heaving into the toilet.

I washed my face and rinsed my mouth. I spent a couple of minutes deep breathing. I was ok.

The moment I opened the door of the washroom I felt the anxiety, dread and shame cloak me again. This frustrated me. *why is my coping so easily shattered as soon as I open the door? Shit, I can't go back in the washroom.* I was mad at myself for being so weak and pathetic.

It's amazing the capacity and speed at which our brains can process thoughts. Looking back, I would describe it like a war in space. My mind felt bombarded with many fast moving memories, and emotions. Paralleled by equal bombardment of reactions & thoughts in the present. I was aware of this duality of experience. I knew for example that the words balled up in the lump in my throat could be released. The right direct question could bring it out. *spit it out, just say it;* I simply could not. A dissociative state occurs when a person is thrown back into a traumatic event. It feels as though the event were happening in that very moment. Some of my dissociative states had me re-experiencing the emotions and body sensations.. While I am feeling childlike and fear is completely overwhelming my ability to breathe, to talk, and to stay adult in the present moment; I was also aware that I was entering into a dissociative state. *I'm just feeling emotions from the past. Breathe, just breathe.* I used grounding techniques like feeling my feet on the floor or the arms of the chair to help stay adult in the present. *I am not a child anymore.*

I heard the vile words in my ear. I felt hot breath on my ears, face and neck. *He's not here. It's safe.* I inhaled the scent of the brute. I knew his scent was not really there. *You're just remembering it. Why can I smell it?* It was a very intense experience. I needed to stop. *It's enough. They have enough.* I tried my best to mask my intense internal struggle seeking to get out of there as quickly as I could. At the end the officer asked, "is there anything I have not asked you that I should have? I could not form a question that would bring out what was still locked inside. The shame of it was too great. I left the interview disappointed with myself for not telling all of the secret things. And for not being able to say the vile words. I had to let it go. I had fulfilled my obligation to the other girls and to my own moral code. I told the truth.

CHAPTER NINE

Hunting for Worms

I could not let it go anymore, I had to confront myself

Going back to my own ordinary life proved to be immensely difficult. My own state of denial reached a point where I could no longer live it. I could not make a case for struggling to keep it up. Some of the pieces from my statement stayed with me and replayed over and over in my head. So did the memories that I had unlocked from the secret file where they were previously contained. By Sunday I was back to smoking and I knew I was in distress again.

I was asked to give an estimate of the number of times I was raped. The question was very disturbing, very confrontational. It confronted my own minimization and denial of the seriousness of my abuse. I could not answer the question.; I did not want to face such a large number. I thought if I got the number wrong my whole testimony would be in question.

I wondered why I always doubted myself, I figured it was because of the minimization and denial of my parents. The numbers of times I was called a psycho or was told that I "must have made that up" Inside of me the truth existed. I decided I wanted to confront every issue that came up in me. I could not let it go anymore, I had to confront my self-doubt.

I was told by a therapist that what I had experienced was torture. The word torture had been mentioned a couple of times over the years during previous therapeutic processes. The word being used offended me greatly. Being of the mindset that the only acceptable use of the word torture applied to POW's or political prisoners. It is disrespectful to those who have suffered obscenities to apply the word to my situation. I was not tortured. It seemed a ridiculous misinterpretation of what torture is.. I dismissed the absurdity of such a suggestion. *People like to blow things out of proportion and make them bigger than they really were. -torture is not what happened to me.* It was one of those words that lingered, floating around in the back of my mind.

Definition of Torture

Webster's:
The act of causing severe physical pain as a form of punishment or as a way to force someone to do or say something

Something that causes mental or physical suffering; a very painful or unpleasant experience

The act of inflicting excruciating pain, as punishment, revenge; as a means of getting a confession; or for sheer cruelty

Oxford:
The action or practice of inflicting severe pain on someone as punishment or in order to force them to do or say something

Sadist:
Someone who gets happiness from hurting others

Victim:
A person who suffers from a destructive or injurious action

After looking it up I had to face the fact that what I experienced matched the definition of torture. The torture I endured was wielded out by a sadist. Saying I was molested as a child was in fact minimizing the truth of my experience; something everybody around me did. Something I had been doing. I had to stop and face the truth.

How many times were you raped? Were objects used to penetrate you; were you sodomized? I don't remember that. instead of, "that didn't happen." *Could I have repressed memories?*

Repressed memories is another hot topic that I avoided like the plague. In the 80's and early 90's many stories came out about therapists bringing out false memories disguised as repressed memories. Oprah had a number of shows on TV regarding the topic. I could imagine that disgustingly debased things could be done to a child such that the child would repress the memory altogether. I did not believe it was true of me. I felt certain I remembered everything and that if by chance something was repressed it was repressed for a reason. I did not need to remember it.

I asked psychologists and psychiatrists about repressed memories because I was starting to believe that it could be possible with me. It was one of those thoughts that had floated around in the back of my mind for years which I never allowed to enter my consciousness.

There was a base, we lived on for one year; that I had no memory of my brother at all. *Why is there a black hole behind the brute's face?* I examined all of my other memories from that base and found that I could accurately describe my school, teacher, classmates, friends events. No memory of my brother abusing me. I had abuse memories from the base prior and from the base after; *is it possible that he stopped for a year?* That was the assumption I had been going by all along. Our family had gotten a dog on that base. I thought my brother had another pastime to occupy him instead of focusing his cruelty on me. I had to face the fact that it was not likely the abuse stopped for a year.Flashbacks, dreams and nightmares came to me slowly at first along with sensations in my body which I had no power over. In the middle of a hot summer day I would get bone penetrating cold chills and begin shivering uncontrollably. My teeth chattered. These chills paralysed me and affected my ability to breathe, to speak and to move. I wrapped myself in blankets and wondered what was happening. It seemed ridiculous to be shivering on a day when everyone else was complaining of the heat.

What was happening to me began to affect my ability to function normally. My sleep was interrupted. I never knew when a flashback would engulf me nor how long it would take me to come out of it. I started avoiding people because I did not want to embarrass myself by having an uncontrollable reaction in front of someone. Nobody needed to see that.

I did my best to seek help. Our systems are lacking in the best approaches to dealing with the after effects of childhood sexual abuse. The more highly trained therapists were out of reach for me financially. The waiting lists to see someone in mental health are long to say the least. I was turned down by five therapists because my financial benefit from my employment for psychological counselling was too low. Therapists felt that I would be left vulnerable because I could not financially sustain sessions for the time period required to deal with my issues.

I was frustrated knowing that I had already opened the can of worms. Worms were escaping in multiple directions. It seemed the story of my life. Never enough money to deal with ill health. The general population has very little understanding of the effects of such a system in Canada. Our health system contributes to the desperation and hopelessness of people and their loved ones.

I ended up being diagnosed with post-traumatic stress disorder and depression. I took my self to the emergency room fearing that I may actually try to do myself harm. Losing control of myself and my reactions was very distressing and humiliating. I was unable to hide from it anymore, unable to employ the strategies I had learned and frustrated that all my years of therapy and hard work had left me in a condition of weakness and vulnerability. I also have this permeating understanding that outside help for the issues that stem from severe childhood abuse or any mental health issue will not suffice. Real change occurs when I become accountable for my own wellness. It's true of each of us. Our systems need to be accountable with us. Chronic poverty followed my life choices no matter how hard I worked. Safe affordable housing was difficult to obtain. Systems should help with those issues. I had several issues to address of which managing my symptoms of PTSD seemed to be the highest priority. Following worms and confronting my issues was significantly difficult.

Among the worms slithering around were the issues of repressed memories which I now was ready to face that I had. The issue of my credibility with myself, the pervasive self-doubt that is me. Facing the seriousness and severity of my childhood neglect and abuse. The fact that I minimized both my abuse and the effects it had on my life. The resulting coping mechanisms which were unhealthy. The fact that I hated myself, had contempt for men, contempt for femininity, contempt for weakness, vulnerability, sexuality and anything less than perfection in terms of my own performance in any area. The fact that my childhood abuse had left me with permanent physical damage and psychological disability. The fact that I have been suffering all of my life and I had become expert at hiding all of it from everyone including myself.

I had made the choice to open the can of worms and now I had to follow it through to the end. I had to find every worm and see where it led, confront every issue head on, deal with each one as best I could and recover whatever I could that had been stolen from me.

My goal was simple: overcome it. All of it.

This was my plan: overcome evil with good.

At home, life was a struggle. I was working too many hours for too little pay. I had three out of four children living with me. Plus two grandchildren, both born under my roof. I had not done well in teaching my children to respect their mother. I came home from work to the house in a mess. I stayed long enough to tidy up and make supper before leaving for the second job. Many times without being able to eat myself. Many evenings I was up late helping my young daughter settle two small children into bed. After which my daughter would need some adult conversation and companionship. I helped to provide as best I could. I was headed for burnout.

I was overworked, following worms, suffering debilitating anxiety and trying to maintain my mask while taking care of the family. I was not feeling well. I took the week off and tried to recover.

I was having flashbacks and nightmares. The events of my childhood were replaying in my head over and over. I was hearing the vile words in my ears.

I wanted to go back to a place of containment. It seemed each week I was confronted by something out of my control which lead back to my childhood. Bumping into a relative of one of the other girls, being asked how my brother was, bumping into an old friend that I had confided in all those years ago.

Thoughts of killing myself began to surface again.

I phoned my therapist and was honest with her about my thoughts. As we discussed my issues I realized the mountain of stress I had been under a long period of time. I needed help to deal with the past surfacing in my life again.Dr. Carolyn Leaf, a renowned neuroscientist explains this phenomenon about the brain; our brain is similar in size and shape to a fist. One part of the brain is not connected directly to the brain mass itself. She explains there are small "bubbles" free floating in front of the brain mass. These floating bubbles are where our free will is located.

Interestingly the brain mass is not connected to any other organ in the body. It connects to the spinal cord and our central nervous system. These free will floating bubbles are the only part of the brain that have a direct connection to another organ. The organ is the human heart. Without the benefit of an education in neuroscience I understood what she was talking about when I heard it.

For me it's that place where my mind and heart meet. The place inside me where I find peace with myself. I know that it's the right decision, the right path. It's the place where I hear my own voice, my own conscience; my moral equilibrium, the place of connection between mind, body and spirit. It's what I follow.

My worm following efforts included dealing with my health, validating myself, and discovering the truth. Seeking the truth has made me a troublemaker. Now that I know the truth; I can see just how much trouble.

Oh, the car is home, her dad must be home. The young girl approached me on the way to school. Grade six. All of the fathers should have been at work. Usually there were no cars. *"Your brother tried to rape me last night."* *"follow me"* I brought her to the house. I knocked on the door. "she has something to tell you" "Tell him what you told me". I walked away and left her standing on the doorstep. *Why did nothing happen? Maybe I didn't bring her to the cop. Did I or didn't I?* I phoned the commanding officer of the base at that time. "Did such a report cross your desk? "No, but I wish it had". I asked the name of the MP on the base. "could such a report have landed on my father's desk before it got to yours? " Humm". A nagging answer to receive.

There were too many things about my childhood experiences that did not make sense. The love story between my parents; my father being so much in love that he changed profession and religion to be with my mother. I saw no such love between them. Every day was robotic. The exact same routines replayed at the exact same time each day. No spontaneity, no conversations, no intimacy, no smiles, no deviating from the routine. My mother despised my father. He did everything he could to keep her content. "We're always watching you they said, we have other people watching you we know everything that you do". They did. *MP's have no jurisdiction off base; they don't operate off base. It's the reason I tried to run off base. Hoping to be found by real police. I was not found by real police. I was found, intimidated and brought back home by men wearing MP uniforms. Did I make that up?* I knew I had not. "You're the mature one; you understand". "Just ignore it." "You'll have to be the one that goes". No discussion, no reasoning, no explanations, no expressions of affection, no expressions of understanding, nor of sympathy. Just dismissal with one line. One statement and that was the end of it. *Had my child been chosen to give flowers to the queen there would have been excitement in the house, acknowledgement.* Pride at having done a perfect curtsey. There would have been photos; a story to pass on. I left a voicemail with dad asking for the spelling of the name of a priest I was fond of and whether my being chosen to present flowers to the queen had anything to do with his position on that base. My father knew that I had started to write this book.

The phone call I received later that evening revealed to me a shocking discovery. My father was drinking at the time of the call. He drinks every evening. The words he spoke were not slurred. They were forceful, intimidating, and loud. My father in full military form accused me of being a mole seeking classified information in order to leak it. I thought he must be suffering from his own PTSD flashback incident.

His verbal tirade took on a life of its own. He mentioned countries that I had never been in. Operations I had no knowledge of. I was fascinated by what he was saying. I would not want to be on the opposite end of an interrogation by him. To say he was intimidating is a gross under-statement. Only in this case, I was not intimidated. He was trying to manipulate me with this fabricated interrogation and I knew it. At one point I interrupted him, "Dad, it's me, Victoria. I was only asking how to spell the priest's name and wondering if my giving flowers to the queen had anything to do your position on the base. "Victoria; pfft," he shouted, "You're no better than all the rest! Seeking classified information in order to leak it! You're all mixed up-you don't know what base we lived on when!" I said, "Dad, I've spent the day researching the base's we lived on, the DND schools I attended. I can give you the exact date queen Elizabeth visited the base". "It was because of girl guides!" he exploded. "And what did you find out about me? "He demanded. "Nothing" I said quietly. *It's as if you didn't exist.* "That's right! It's classified!" "Ok, Dad. Sorry to have bothered you. I got it. It was because of girl guides". "Yes, it was because of girl guides" he confirmed, calmer now. "That's all I needed, Dad, I'll let you go now. Hope you relax and enjoy the rest of your evening". "Ok, Victoria; love you. It was because of girl guides". "I love you too Dad, I got it. Goodnight. Talk to you again soon".

I knew my father was intelligence. I thought it had to do with decoding secret messages during the cold war, the Cuban missile crisis, whatever else our country faced. Canadians forget just how intense that period was for our country's defence forces. I understand the tension from the period because I lived it in my home. I began to do more worm finding. I was determined to find the truth. I was not sure where to start so I began by looking up acronyms that I remembered from my youth. Military acronyms. Acronyms that I will not be able to mention here but which led me to some interesting information on the internet. I noted where the information came from, who had written the articles. I started printing off a few I found the most interesting. One article described my father exactly though the article's writer could not discover the name of his subject. Too many facts lined up for the pieces to have been a coincidence. Or to have been discussing a person other than my father. Some facts are verifiable; and my life, where I lived and when, verified too much in this article for me to have been mistaken. I researched my father's military service and the base's we lived on. I researched the DND schools I had attended. I wondered about my father. He was detachment commander on some base's. He has plaques on his wall, awards that include his title. I could find no mention of him on any of the base's where we lived. There were photos and bios of other servicemen from those base's. I was examining the worm of self-doubt. It was not me I should be doubting-it was my father. I made a bold move. I telephoned the author of the article. I thought to discover what I had come to suspect. That my father had somehow covered up the incident with the other young girl. What I went away with was a whole lot more than I could ever have imagined.

On May 21, 1954 my father made a decision to enlist in the Royal Canadian Navy, first as a reservist then later becoming regular force. In fact, he was too young to join but he lied about his age on the application. Nobody bothered to check, or if they did check, they ignored the fact of his youth. He told me once that he was recruited into intelligence service right out of his first test scores having scored so well. He waited until 10 years after his retirement to talk about being a cryptographer, a piece of information that was classified for 10 years. Prior to that my understanding was my father was in communications, a radio operator by trade. I knew he had some involvement in sending and receiving communications from Russia during the cold war. He identifies those who served during those years as cold war vets not peacetime vets. *Calling them peacetime vets diminishes their service to our country in a time when peace was an illusion* he says. As I began to gather evidence of what I suspected happened on one particular base I began to uncover the real reason my heart dictated *protect the work* when I left home at 16 in 1984.

In his book, "The Haunting Memories of War, a memoir of father and son"; co-author Roger Klare details parallels he finds between his father's WW II experiences and incidents that occurred in his own childhood. Something he calls the parallax view. On page 165 he says, "My father's haunting memories of war had been transformed into my own haunting memories. Such is the power of war and memory. Discovering these connections and making sense of them has taken many years of effort. Yet I have felt compelled to find these connections, as understanding the how and why of things has always been a goal of mine. It comes naturally from my lifetime interest in science."

Though I claim no such natural interest in science, reading the passage corroborated the parallels between my father's service and my childhood experiences. Following my worm trail led me to see several others. I spoke by telephone to retired military intelligence personnel and writers of military and investigative reporting backgrounds. I spoke to former CO's and MP's from bases I lived on. Veterans who had known my father and worked with him during their service. After I gathered the evidence I needed to confront my father with my suspicions I did so. With tears in his eyes he made his confession. "What can I do about it now except say that I'm sorry". "Don't you think I worried? I was glad when you left home, at least you were away from him." Discovering connections and making sense of them can bring understanding to an experience.

In the years following WW II, Canada had an intelligence strategy of arranging marriages. Creating families by way of adopting children in order to imbed agents into military installations both in Canada and abroad. I was adopted into one such family in 1969. Finding out that my family was artificially created was gob-smacking, mind blowing and unbelievable. At the same time clarity came to the parallel pieces that began falling into place as though they were part of a magnificent, complex puzzle. The made up love story between my parents. The reason I saw no such love between them. The adopting of children roughly six years later; another arrangement, "We found out we couldn't have children so we decided to adopt". No mention of wanting children because there was no wanting of children. Our family was a cover story to hide my father's true position. Our family was a job. Perhaps the reason for the intensity of my mother's contempt for my father. Motherhood was a job she never wanted.

My father's "recruitment" into intelligence service destined him to signing a contract which bound him to secrecy until death. Our family was non-political in nature. Politics were never discussed at home. I was hit with a yard stick on the fingers in grade 8 because I could not tell the teacher which political party my father supported. My father signed away his right to vote before he was eligible to vote. He pledged allegiance to the government Canada, regardless of party in power. My father has never voted but diligently served the Department of National Defense. His silence continues to do so.

Military Police came off a base to locate a missing runaway; in reality men who belonged to a secret lodger unit. Fully supplied and operationally independent. Not MP's. Collaborating with their detachment commander to keep things contained. Men on one base collaborated to cover up the crimes of a son in order to protect the father's work. Dad told me of the many times containment was needed in the previous decades. Covering up infidelity of husbands and of wives. Covering men with drinking problems, gambling problems, financial and other "embarrassments" All in the name of secrecy of mission. Having been brainwashed as they were. The atmosphere these men found themselves in was not as romantic as the recruiter suggested I suspect. They ended up in an atmosphere of heavy responsibility with little direction, not knowing who to trust. Rank has little meaning when it comes to the highest levels of secrecy within the establishment.

I've had the privilege of speaking frankly with men about what it was like to serve in lodger units in such a time in our history. They were lodged everywhere. In radio shacks on ships. My father told me stories of his early days in the diplomatic courier service. He talked about the tension involved in carrying the red cases. I asked him if while there he took time to see the sights. "Honestly Victoria, I just wanted to get the hell out of there." It was nerve wracking. He talked about various missions to find and destroy clandestine listening devices and microphones. As I listen to him I can't imagine what that must have been like. He talked about other intriguing operations. He explained the different communication systems that came into service such as telex and OCAMS (Ottawa Communications Automated Message Switch), NOCAMS (New OCAMS) and the testing protocol of Signet Communications.

What he remembers most are the people who were closest to him. One guy on his team had to be fired due to the actions of his children. They were stealing; on and off base. A guy's wife was having an affair with one of dad's men and refused to end it. My father couldn't end the affair, his man tried to end it. My father could not transfer his own man-he transferred the other guy. The innocent husband with the cheating wife. Incidents like these keep him up at night.

He finally told me the reason for his distrust of the Royal Canadian Mounted Police. Initially he was opposed to the RCMP being added to the Veteran's Affairs Act programs. During these discussions I used my father's own words against his argument that RCMP did not belong among the ranks of the retired vets. One of his most famous lines is, "A veteran is a veteran is a veteran" meaning no matter the service they provided, they were equal under the VAC Act and should all be treated with equal dignity, diligence and respect. I defended the RCMP citing that they carry weapons, risk their lives daily in the streets of Canada, and they are a national force. I joke that the job of a constable is more dangerous than that of a military radio operator. Eventually he came to respect the RCMP and serves them as diligently as he would any other vet. His distrust came from a long ago incident in intelligence service. Soon after the RCMP had been brought into the military intelligence community a mole was discovered within their hierarchy. That person was eventually cleared but my father had been part of the mission that uncovered the mole. He was convinced of the mole and never fully trusted any RCMP after that. I finally understood the source of our many debates.

My father told me he sat down with two other men as was the custom whenever there was a "problem". They sat together and discussed what the problem was and how they were going to handle it. After that they contained it and denied it ever existed. My father would destroy any remaining evidence of the problem. This method was how they came to the decisions they did with regards to my brother's activities on one particular Canadian Forces Base. My brother was not charged in the sexual assault of a young girl. His involvement was known. As was his involvement in other crimes such as home invasions, theft, drugs and vandalism. I knew nothing of my brother's activities outside what he was doing to me. Until a girl in my class came up to me. They covered it up. Three men I respect. Now I understand what happened. I did my best to help her. The system failed us. How can I possibly judge such men? They did what they thought was best at the time. The cost of our freedom in Canada continues to be staggering. The US and Canada alone share

80 treaty level defense agreements and over 250 memoranda of intent on defense and intelligence. My father spied on international enemies, allies and domestic Canadians. He spied on his own government, his own men and of course me. His main task became destroying everything that threatened exposure of his secret role in a sect of the Department of National Defense or Department of Foreign Affairs and International Trade, or the Communications Security Establishment, or the Privy Council. His position remains a mystery. They covered it up. I get it. It was what they did. I wonder what happened to the girl. *Am I the only one?*

CHAPTER TEN

Destroying Deception

There is something justified in
being a victim. It wasn't my fault.

I've learned a thing or two about war. No war is worth the cost. Sometimes it's better to end it. The war we should focus our attention on is the war we rage against ourselves. It spills over and hurts others. My heart spoke to me one day: *You are wearing masculinity and layers of self-protection. You have contempt for men and have been at war with men for thirty-six years.*

I don't hate men. I don't like to show vulnerability in front of men but that does not mean that I have contempt for men. *Does it?* In a review of my life I saw what my war and contempt looked like.

Contempt is subtle. When I was a young I had to beat the boys. Beat them in anything I could win. Climbing trees, catching frogs, reading, writing, speaking, school tests, swimming, physical challenges, sports, shooting & drill in cadets. I couldn't beat them all but boy did I try. I beat as many as I could. In lifeguarding I had to be the best. I had to be the fastest, the strongest and the smartest. I was always happy to beat a boy at anything. When any man communicated poorly, I was there to communicate better. When any man displayed a lack of leadership, I was there to lead better. I hated not being able to do something and needing a man to it for me.

One day my furnace ran out of oil so I had to go buy a can of furnace oil. No problem. Pour the oil into the pipe that feeds the furnace. No problem. Bleed the line. Problem. I could not get the nut off the bolt. I tried everything. I used all of my might. It just would not budge! I worked on it forty-five minutes during my lunch break. After work I tried again, no luck. I had to break down and call my ex-husband, "Could you come over and loosen this nut for me so I can bleed the line to the furnace?" He came, and with one turn of the vice grip had the stupid thing off! My rage was masked in gratitude covering over my indignation. Grrrrr! Contempt.

War on the other hand involves strategy; strategy for defence and strategy for offense. Here are some examples of what my war looked like.

Never allow an unknown male to help with anything. See an unknown male walking down the street, cross to the other side. Count the number of unknown males in the room. If the number is too high, do not enter the room. Never put an unknown male between me and the door. Never let my guard down in front of a man and never show vulnerability.

If you were a male in high school with me and expressed any interest in me beyond friendship you received a response in direct correlation to your approach. If the approach was calm and respectful, "I really like you will you go out with me?" My response would be calm and respectful, "I can't go out with you, and I don't like you the same way". If any male made an approach that was physical or assertive in any way the response was physical and aggressive, "don't ever f___ing touch me or I'll rip your f___ing face off!"

Never be in the same place with the combination of males and alcohol. Alcohol makes any male unpredictable and dangerous.

I've made up believable excuses. I have had men removed from social functions, work related events, weddings and the like.

I was always aware of males around me. I was constantly watching their expressions waiting for danger. I hated that males are bigger than me. I hated that males are stronger than me. I was always at war.

As much as I was at war with men, I was at war with women too. I hated femininity. I hated girls as much as I hated boys. I couldn't stand girls. I could not relate to the girls in high school. At lunch time in the cafeteria the girls would be talking about boys, clothes, make up and TV shows they watched. I was concerned about surviving, working and paying rent. I could care less about shopping for clothes or what was on sale where. I could care less about who liked which boy and I certainly did not care about what was on TV last night.

I couldn't discuss school work. When you are lying on your bedroom floor after being raped you don't get up and finish your homework. I didn't care about homework. I did only what I needed to do to get by.

By grade ten I rarely went to the cafeteria for lunch. I started avoiding the masses as much as I could without attracting notice.

Women are manipulative, deceptive and they use their sexuality against males. Women are backstabbing usurpers. I didn't trust them either. I had three basic charges against men. Charge one; men abuse their authority. Charge two; men abdicate their positions of authority. Charge three; men abandon their women and children. Look around and see the numbers of verbal, physical and sexual assaults perpetrated by males against females. Look around and see how many violations occur from males in positions of authority. Look around and see the vast number of households headed by females. I felt secure in my judgement of men. I would have preferred to be a man. What I wouldn't have given to be six feet, three inches tall, two hundred, twenty-eight pounds and male. *Nobody would hurt me then!* I came a lot closer to the two hundred and twenty-eight pounds than I ever did six foot three.

Wearing layers of self-protection is easy to see from the outside. It looks like excess body fat and unattractive features. My unconscious strategy was to be as fat and ugly as possible so that I would not attract attention.

Wearing masculinity meant something about the clothing I chose to wear. I wore dark colors; masculine lines and baggy stuff. I did not wear anything feminine, pretty or pink. I did not wear jewelry or high heeled shoes. I did not wear make-up. I did not sit, stand, walk or move in a feminine way. I went so far as to have surgery to reduce the size of my breasts. at the age of 21, *get these things off me*. I mutilated my own body in an attempt to avoid femininity.

Separating myself became my way of life. Separating me from others began as a subconscious survival mechanism. It turned into a life of war, contempt, and self-protection.

I had to face my true self wondering, *so now what?*. I saw myself. I was not happy with what I saw. On the outside most people would call me friendly. Most would say I am kind or nice. I have avoided conflict whenever I could. I considered myself to be a decent person. I started out innocent. There is something justified in being a victim. It wasn't my fault.

I have this tiny little voice inside me that would cry out weakly at random times. It always sounded far away, *I'm innocent* . As I was reviewing my life of war and contempt the voice cried out again, *I'm innocent.* I thought *what exactly am I guilty of?* When I asked Jesus into my life I asked Him to forgive me of my sin. My sin was easy to see. I had a history of sin. It was sin when I wanted to kill my brother. It was sin when I tried to cure myself of hating the idea of sex. But I didn't kill my brother and my strategy for curing my self was just a lost kid trying to cope. My reaction was understandable. I made mistakes in parenting but who doesn't. I followed my moral code and was ethical. I had both sin and iniquity. I had some difficulty understanding what iniquity was. The word iniquity is most commonly used to describe a group of people or a nation. When found in an individual, it is being in a state of constant sin. I was actually in a state of constant sin which was harmful to other people.

I'll give you one example of my iniquity. My hating femininity affected my oldest daughter in this way. As a child she was a girly girl. She loved everything feminine. She loved the color pink. She loved to play with hair. She created pretty hair styles on her dolls. She loved putting on play makeup and fingernail polish. She was feminine. As she grew and started to develop I would not allow her to choose feminine clothing. I didn't want her wearing jewelry or make-up. I didn't want her to look attractive in any way. If she came downstairs wearing something that would attract attention, I was terrified. Panic would rise up in me. I would send her up to change. For her to wear I purchased what was comfortable for me. I wanted her to look in a way that was comfortable for me.

"You shouldn't go out wearing that, high heels attract attention" "Mom, what happened to you isn't going to happen to me". "But it could if you wear that". "Mom, it won't". "Yes, it could". I asked her if we could compromise. If you wear high heels make sure your shoulders are covered. If your shoulders are uncovered; wear flats. Tone down the make-up and cover the cleavage. Her make- up and jewelry were not out of line. Her high heeled shoes while driving me crazy were fashionable and appropriate for the young women her age. What sounded reasonable to me lead to many battles. The more I tried to make my point, the harder she tried to make hers. My trying to protect in reality was me communicating to her; don't be pretty, don't be attractive, don't be feminine. As if she could be anything but. The damage I inflicted to her body image and sense of self-worth is staggering. That's the basic problem with being an innocent victim; our protective measures hurt others. Our reactions to the world around us are out of order and out of balance. We react to everything around us. Our reactions are constant. I was in a constant state of reacting poorly Obviously I did not intend to hurt my daughter; nevertheless, I hurt my daughter, my other children, my parents, my partners and many people who I crossed paths with.

My choices in relationships are another example. I identified with wounded men and chose them as my partners. I understood why the men I chose reacted to life with anger. I found qualities in the men that were easy to love. I followed the lessons instilled in me. *Don't react. Ignore it when someone violates you.* I thought I was doing right.

I minimized the abuse that happened to me and accepted it as normal. I minimized the effect that those relationships had on my children. I told myself that they didn't see or experience the abuse that happened to me in my marriage. I told myself that having a father figure and having a family unit was more important than living a peaceful life.

I did not believe in divorce. I thought I was doing right by staying in abusive relationships. I was wrong. I stayed because I believed the things that were said to me, that nobody else would love me. I believed that I did not deserve anything better. I believed that I would never find anything better. I believed that all relationships and marriages had abuse. I did not believe that anything better existed. I was wrong. I stayed in unhealthy relationships far too long. I stayed because I was convinced. I stayed because I was afraid. I stayed because I was afraid of being alone. I stayed because it was hard to get out. I stayed because I was trying to have a father for my children.

I was wrong.

I was trying so hard to have a father for my children because I pitied them. Mothers should not pity their children. My reactions were wrong thinking. My reactions were understandable and normal. The effects of my childhood abuse; yet my wrong thinking created chaos, disorder, fear, despair and hopelessness for me and for my children. I am accountable. It's a burden I have to live with for the rest of my life.

My war, my contempt, my self-protection; all of it hurt other people. My choices affected so many others. I hurt the ones I love the most.

There is a saying in Christianity that comes from the Bible; the truth will set you free. I believe it is true. What I have learned is that confronting the truth about me sets me free. The truth is gentle with us when we are hurting and gentle with us when trying to confront our methods of self-protection. The gentleness is the reason that the truth is so easy to deny. The little nag of conscience that we so easily justify to ourselves or dismiss. Condemnation is the thing we are most afraid of, that if we are guilty we are also condemned.

If I have no fear of being condemned I need not fear being guilty. The first step in solving any problem is acknowledging the problem exists. Understanding that the problem of being me was not something I needed to condemn myself for was not an easy challenge.

How to go end a war that was habit. A way of being. It seemed a huge challenge. Reclaiming my femininity and sexuality left me wondering what those words meant.

I contacted the society I called when I first left home. I asked if there may be a report with my name on it from 1984. There was. The lady I met with in 1984 kept her vow to me not to report what I had said to the police or to document any specific details of what I had to say. I had not forgotten her. Her name was at the bottom of the report. Nobody at the society knew who she was. I realized that she may have a different name after so many years. I asked God to help me find her. Within two weeks I found her. She lived across the country but the next week she was coming back to Eastern Canada for a vacation. I met with her. She remembered me. Meeting with her again after so many years was wonderful for me. It was very validating and healing to be able to share more of my details with her. I heard details from her side of the story. The first thing she did was apologise for not helping me more. She saw something in me, a stubbornness, that she felt comfortable with, believing I would be ok. "Where there's a will, there's a way" she quoted "what I saw in you was a will, a determination, a strength", she said. I felt validated.

I'm accountable. For my will and my ways. Victims must be accountable. We must be if we want to be part of the healing process. The justice process. Justice for me is my wellness. I am responsible for it. I have done all I can to understand me. I take responsibility for my actions. *What can I do about it now? Change it.*

I connected to past friends former teachers and educators, boys to whom I had been nasty, friends in whom I had confided. I found a counsellor generous enough to take me on knowing I had limited ability to pay for the services I required.

Not every worm I followed lead to successful or happy results. Some led to the brick walls of denial and withdrawal. I don't want to minimize the effect of running head on into a brick wall. There were many days I was left injured, debilitated, emotional, desperate, afraid and feeling very isolated. Many days I contemplated whether I would ever know the truth. Or be able to recover control over my- self. Many days I contemplated whether my life was worth living at all.

These days were very dark. I isolated myself especially from my children and acquaintances.

Survivor:
Someone with great powers of endurance; someone who shows a great will to live or a great determination to overcome difficulties and carry on

Femininity and sexuality was another matter altogether.

What a privilege it is to be discovering what my sexuality at this time; after the age of forty. I have such an intimate relationship with sexual dysfunction. I thought of myself as perverse. I was well into my thirty's before I experienced an orgasm. It's was my husband's idea that I should add climaxing to my list.

So I did. In order to climax I had to retreat into a fantasy state. The fantasies included violence intimidation, coercion & control. Professionals have told me that rape fantasy is common among women. Women who have not ever been raped-fantasise about it.

Fantasy and reality are two different things. My debate was not whether rape fantasy is right or wrong; my issue was that the state I put myself into was a dissociative state. A dissociative state means I was not mentally, intellectually or emotionally present during love making with my husband.

It's a very natural response. Except that I became an expert at recreating the brain link between sex and violence in my own mind. I used fantasy while pleasuring myself. My mind had its own way of creating stimuli for me. It led down a harmful path. I don't write this stuff easily. My hope is to open understanding, maybe dialogue, maybe individual change. A natural response for which I am accountable. *Accountable to who? To me.*

Lots of people use various forms of self-harm. I'm lucky not to have gone down the path too far with sexual self-harm. I did penetrate myself once with an inappropriate object. No, I don't want to tell you about it.

Everybody wants to know. Even the people who shy away hope to discover the answer discreetly. Readers wondering, "What did you use, what did you do?" My problem is not in telling you what I did. My problem is you're asking the wrong question for the wrong reason. .

I used a broom handle the first time. I couldn't think what else to use and I didn't have anything else available to me at the time.

Writing that line reminded me my mother thought the use of tampons meant a loss of virginity. I had this need, not desire; but like an addict needs a fix. I had this need to have something inside me. It wasn't big enough around and it didn't hurt enough. I tried harder and harder until it produced pain and bleeding. Then I felt relief. I was thinking it was what I deserved, being injured and bleeding, for being so perverse. Knowing that just like alcohol or a drug I could become addicted to the feeling it created.

I would have continued on that path of sexual self -harm had I not worked in a bathing suit seven days a week. I feel very privileged to have escaped that trap knowing so many of us do not. Sexual self-harm is one of the effects of childhood sexual trauma and so very many people live with shameful secrets about what they do to themselves. Isolated in it, and unable to find a way out.

Instead of sexual self-harm; in my mid-thirty's I became a compulsive masturbator and I created horrific violent fantasy in order to achieve multiple orgasms. I didn't use objects. Sexual dysfunction is sexual dysfunction.

I cried many times after sexual intercourse with my husband too. It just wasn't the way I wanted to be, using sick fantasy to climax. I had to battle with those thoughts of right versus wrong, and of normal versus deviant sexual behavior.

A friend suggested I date men from a particular profession because I could be sure I would not be with a sexual deviant. I replied, "I'm a sexual deviant". She said mine didn't count. I know she said it because she has compassion and empathy for victims. Victims can be justified because we were wronged.

I believe in personal responsibility and my sexual dysfunction counts to me.

The privilege of choice is my blessing now. I get to choose my sexuality and I know it. I refuse to live with sexual dysfunction. I know that I have a choice; many choices about what I want my sexuality to be. I get to examine my sexuality from all angles and figure out where each mindset came from. Much of my mindset came from my Roman Catholic, religious upbringing. Much of it came from my trauma, some of it came from neglect, some from my militaristic duty and compliance mindset and most of it came from fear and shame.

I've had male friends and colleagues ask, "My wife won't make love to me with the lights on, would you talk to her?" Don't ask me how that question comes up because I will tell you that there is an un-seen recognition and connection that occurs when victims encounter each other. It just comes up; and yes, the spouses and partners of sexually violated people become victims too. Almost everyone is a victim of sexual shame in some form or another.

I remember those days when shame had power over me and I'm so happy to be free of the shackles of shame. It took a long time and lots of difficult work but I was able to choose my way out of it.

The first time I was asked, "How do you feel about your sexuality?" I was in my early thirty's. I was offended at the question. I didn't think of myself as a sexual being at the time. I thought of myself as a wife; I did my duty.

What the fuck kind of question is that? What does sexuality mean anyway?

Now I know I can examine how I think about sex, why I think that way and whether I want to continue thinking the same. Therapy can fuck you up if you let it. It's another reason personal accountability is essential to wellness. I was advised to have many lovers, to try lesbianism, to masturbate freely, to watch pornography, to fantasize freely, and to explore my fantasies freely. Various counselors, group sessions and therapy types introduce options. What a confusing array of choices I was given.

Confronting my sexual dysfunction meant I had to start with kissing.

I had to start with actually looking at a penis. I wondered if I could smell and touch a penis while staying present in the moment in mind and body. I was deciding whether or not whether I wanted to try and put a penis in my mouth.

The great thing about therapy is that it can help. I was a middle aged, physically disabled single mother living in a small town.

I had to think about whether I wanted to have sex outside of marriage. Whether I thought it was right or wrong, whether it was right or wrong in general or whether it was right or wrong for me. I had to examine my moral code.

There were health issues to consider, moral issues in question and embarrassment at having so little understanding of my sexuality at my age. I turned to my ex-husband for help. I chuckle at the debate raging in my mind about how to ask him.

Should I just call him up? And say...what exactly? Because I am sly by nature, I wanted to call him up and say, "I want to suck your cock".

I could not say those words at that time because I was too repressed and I knew we had to start with, "Can I look at your penis?"

I was dying inside of embarrassment. I knew if I called him it would end up something like, "hi...uh...aah...umhmm...I think I called the wrong number by mistake, how are you anyway?

My other option was to just wait until he made a sexual advance. My final option was to tell him the truth. It was the most difficult option to imagine. It wasn't like he knew nothing; he knew I was molested in my childhood. He never heard many of the details; many of the details didn't get uttered from my lips until I was at the police station.

Having the whole debate in my mind was funny, I thought it was hilarious even to be thinking such things and I knew whichever approach I used he would not turn me down. I knew I could conquer my own shame because I had found one part of my sexuality with which I was at peace.

I was at peace with wanting to give oral sex; there was no longer lingering religious ideas about oral sex being wrong, bad or shameful, I only had to conquer the trauma effects. I knew I could. In the end nature assisted me with my approach to my ex-husband. I woke up extremely frustrated and angry one Friday morning. I didn't know what to do with myself. I had this desire to get drunk. I wanted to hear the sound of glass shattering. I told him how I was feeling. I wanted to go to the woods with a bat and shatter glass to smithereens. Lucky for me he happened to have a box of glass dishes that he had no use for. He understood my need to have protection if I was drinking without my having to say it. He was very obliging to drive me to the liquor store and to Walmart for a bat. Walmart had none so we settled on a hockey stick instead. We headed to a perfect spot in the woods.

He set up an obstacle course of glass for me to smash while I started with my first couple of drinks. I watched his creativity as he found ways of placing various glass objects in trees, bushes, on logs at varying heights and depths. When he was finished and I looked at it, it was an amazing gesture of caring. I had great appreciation for his work. It could have been crappy; I was already drunk. I asked him to ensure that every piece of glass I smashed was picked up afterwards so nature would be left intact after my tirade.

I set to work with the hockey stick allowing myself to vocalize my anger while I made my way through my obstacle course smashing mugs with all my might and plates with less voracity. I savored the sound that I wanted to hear. The sound had life in it.

When I finally finished smashing everything I could with the hockey stick I watched him diligently pick up the pieces. I was drunk, exhausted and had released quite a lot of anger but something wasn't finished yet.

My ex graciously pulled out his bb gun and set up a Pepsi can for me to shoot at. Since he had trouble hitting the can he thought to challenge me by saying hit each of the letters in order without missing a shot.

I don't remember how I started or how long it took, but in between shots, drinks and cigarettes my story started pouring out of me with all of the emotion it had in it. I paused a few times, asking if he really wanted to hear. He quietly said, "I'm still listening" which was what I needed to hear in order to continue. I don't know how long it took but I finished before shooting at the last "I".

After making the shot I laid the gun on the ground and started to crawl away. He asked me where I was going, "I'm going to die now, just clean up the mess, go away and leave me here". Instead he came over to me and tried to hug me but I couldn't handle that and said, "Don't-don't touch me, leave me alone" I turned away from him as I started to sob uncontrollably. He wrapped his arms around me and I didn't have any strength to fight him and he whispered in my ear, "Its ok, I'm still here, just let it out". He whispered all of the right words into my ear as I sobbed, "You're ok, you're safe, I'm here, I've got you, I'm not letting go" and he positioned us so that I was cradled within the safety of his chest, arms and head.

I refused to be ashamed anymore.

If you are a woman who is unable to have sex with the lights you may be living in a state of shame. Shame is an enemy of self love.

Fear is an enemy of love. I was so afraid when I wanted to conquer my aversion to penises. I challenged my fear and overcame it. Discuss it. Have the discussion in the dark.

That is the hardest part, talking about it. Prolonged exposure therapy has worked very well for me because I decided to embrace the process. The worst of my imagined fears never happened.

Over the years I have spoken with counsellors and have attended group therapy for survivors of childhood sexual abuse. The sessions are good. Not every counsellor fits every client. If you've tried it and it didn't seem a good fit, try again. I learned strategies in counselling that helped me deal with flashbacks (flashes of memory that come to your mind out of nowhere in unpredictable moments), nightmares and general anxiety. I learned strategies for relaxation. I learned the names of my coping techniques like disassociation (going somewhere else in your mind while being abused). I learned that I was the same as other victims of abuse. I learned that re-victimization (getting into other abusive relationships) is a common side effect of childhood abuse. I was not alone in my reactions to the circumstances of my life.

I learned that I can turn away from my wrong thinking patterns and I can find new ways to think. Often I have found that I need help to acquire new thinking patterns and I am no longer afraid of seeking the help I need.

While counselling is good and can be effective if you really put effort into learning, none of what I learned really healed the wounds of my heart. Even after all that I had learned I still felt ugly, defiled, damaged, untrustworthy, unlovable and unworthy. Counselling could not give me back any of the things that I had lost.

CHAPTER ELEVEN

Experiencing Living

the battle is won by a simple
strategy

At times I would like to rage knowing the effect of early childhood trauma on me. Knowing the effect of my trauma on my children & grandchildren. Termed intergenerational transference of trauma. Scientific research has found that trauma affects every cell in the human body leaving a psychological imprint, a biological imprint, a neurological imprint, a chemical imprint, and a physiological imprint. I would add a spiritual imprint as well.

An imprint that eradicates identity, security, attachment and normal brain development. Multiple risk factors diminishing capacity for developing healthy relationships. Risk factors include severe isolation, depersonalization or the loss of self and dissociation. Diminished capacity for educational success, chronic poverty, inadequate housing in unsafe neighborhoods, poor diet and increased health risks for physical injury, mental health issues, drug and alcohol abuse, gambling, sexual dysfunction and various forms of self-harm including death by suicide.

I have suffered these effects and the added intrusions of depression, anxiety, debilitating flashbacks, nightmares and a pervasive loss of connection to everything and everyone. I suffered a complete lack of self-esteem to the degree that I was convinced I was a fraud, a liar and totally crazy.

I slipped through every crack in every system that Canada has designed to help people with diminished capacity or opportunity. Starting with Community Services Child Protection to Adoption Services to CPP disability and Widow's Allowance up to and including mental health services to this day. Despite all of my attempts to self-protect and to seek out help in a variety of forms; I was absolutely alone in dealing with the after effects of my childhood trauma. These continued in my life as re-traumatization until I finally understood enough at the age of forty-five to begin to hope that I could make significant changes in my life that help my life seem worth the effort and cost of living it.

I could rage but why should I? I was very clear with myself before going to make a statement to the police. I would encourage anyone to examine yourself first and be sure of your goals for the justice you seek.

I've sat with many young girls, women and men raped or assaulted at home, in school, in college, in university, and at work, at church, in sports. I've heard every reason for not coming forward. Lingering is the question, *Could you live with yourself if it happened again tonight?* I have endured the process of going through it.

In coming forward I had three main goals: to acknowledge the truth and its effects, to confront every issue that came up and to tell my story. Those were my personal goals. Justice is something else.

If I am able to accept and deal appropriately with my anxiety, depression and chronic thoughts of suicide, if I am able to accept my femininity . It's my wellness. Punishing someone else has nothing to do with it. Revealing the truth does. I agree with a statement from a client interviewed in the book "Feeling Unreal" (Daphne Simeon, 2006) who said, "I'd rather have cancer than this", "With a disease that people know you get some degree of empathy. But if you try to explain this, people either think you're crazy or completely self- absorbed and neurotic. So you keep your mouth shut and suffer silently". Such is the case in Canada today.

Intrinsically, human beings learn the value of suffering when we experience it. With that comes an intrinsic value for life. I wonder if our government is still creating artificial families. If so whether there a plan in place to deal with negative after effects on the participants. We need to be able to trust our government to do right by those they enlist; especially if they suffer an injury or have been taken from orphanages.

The buck stops somewhere on this one; and not on the fall guy. Who should I blame and rage at in my case? The brute who abused me, the parents who ignored it, or the government that created the circumstances in the first place?

I do not condemn the actions of our government in my life circumstances, I have chosen not to. Why? Because I do not have the courage, strength or intellect to sit in any of their hot seats. I pay great homage to all those who sit in the hot seats, those in leadership roles, those who make decisions, and those who bear arms because I have heard their stories and the stories of their families. I know what it takes from them and whether the person is good, bad or ugly in the hot seat; they all started out like me-innocent.

I could jump on many bandwagons, but my heart isn't in it. Just like it wasn't in being an elite swim coach or a professional actress. My heart is with those who suffer. My heart is with humanity, with life, with hope in eternity and with God.

My heart is with those caught in the traps of domestic violence, child abuse, neglect, rape, sexual assault, illness, injury and disease. With their partners and families. My heart is with social workers, teachers, counsellors, police officers, lawyers and judges who suffer lack of understanding, funding, training, guidance and case law to deal effectively with the scope of it.

I will not jump on any of these bandwagons. I refuse to hate, I refuse to judge, I refuse to condemn. I'd rather laugh.

I'd rather remember the ice fishing story and tell you about that. We can share a chuckle. Jumping on bandwagons can be someone else's occupation. I am occupied with maintaining my wellness, following the voice of my heart and hearing the symphony of life on earth.

I can judge no one.

I am humbled when I hear the sound of suffering or when I see it, or feel it. It is part of the human experience; it's wiping your spouse's private and vulnerable parts when they are dying, or telling a person that their child has died; or a child, that their parent has died, it's illness and injury and pain.

I hear the sound of heaven in my heart. It is the sound of the response to suffering. It is the sound of life and it is a symphony of victory.

The victory symphony can be heard on earth. It's the sound of a baby breathing, waves crashing, birds singing and people laughing. It's the sound of love.

The sound of justice is wholeness and my victory is in wellness achieved not by compartmentalization or repression or evasion or seeking revenge or the punishment of another but by embracing the suffering and covering it over with love. Starting with self love.

I have been asked so many times as I'm sure other former lifeguards will attest to being asked, "How many lives have you saved". I worked thirty years in aquatics and I cannot give an answer to that question. I know that if the answer were just one; it would make the thirty years' worth it.

There are so many "ones" in isolation. If you are, come out. Come out of isolation.

I refuse to hate. I refuse to live in an un-healthy state. I refuse to be silent. I refuse to stay still; I refuse not to grow as a person, as a woman, as a sexual being, as a mother, a teacher, a mentor, a coach, an encourager, and a humanitarian. I can hear my own symphony; the symphony of my life.

I hear the sound of me; a child with a broken heart, a broken body and a broken mind. It has within it the sounds of rebellion, anger and injustice yet those sounds are covered over by tenacity, compassion and empathy.

Unimaginable to my mind is my own response to my suffering. I cannot comprehend it. My response to my suffering is to forgive those who caused it, love those who understand it and give hope to those who need it.

True love exists all around us, between us and within us. Human beings are the embodiment of true love and we must learn to give and receive self-love if we wish to be that embodiment of love.

I have always loved the quote by Nelson Mandela;

> "Our deepest fear is not that we are inadequate. Our deepest fear is that we are powerful beyond measure. It is our light, not our darkness that frightens us most. We ask ourselves, "Who am I to be brilliant, gorgeous, talented and fabulous?" Actually, who are you not to be? You are a child of God. You're playing small does not serve the world. There is nothing enlightened about shrinking so that people won't feel insecure around you. We were born to make manifest the glory of God that is within us. It's not just in some of us; it's in all of us. And when we let our own light shine, we unconsciously

give other people permission to do the same. As we are liberated from our own fear, our presence automatically liberates others."

As I write, birds are chirping at my window, I can hear wind, smell rain and feel its dampness. I can still feel emptiness and loneliness from my childhood. At this moment it is a memory covered over in love for myself but tomorrow I could be wrapped in the stickiness of the deception that emptiness lives forever. I can lose a day being human on earth; suffering self-pity or self-hate.

I hear the sound of victory when my life, intersects with another and creates something good. Like the kids in swim class, or the grandparents.

I hear the sound of their accomplishments, their hopes and their dreams. Become a part of it. Share yourself.

Embracing the truth about myself and my family, history, heritage, my journey and my life; embracing the world around me means I am not destroyed by it.

Everyone has a story.

I have been privileged to hear stories from people all over the world. I have participated in peer counselling of other survivors. I have heard personal stories of atrocities committed in conflict zones. One person told me of becoming a child soldier. Another told me of watching their entire family being killed in front of them. One told me of walking from one African country to another to escape violence. I have read about the tortures of people during wars. I have seen images of destruction on the news, in documentaries. I have heard from the lips of those who serve just how perverse our world can be. I have not suffered such things. I can't even imagine it.

The horror of their stories does not lessen the impact of mine. Neither does my story lessen the impact of yours.

Some have told me of their anger and reaction to a violation that seemed so much smaller in scale, a husband who spoke disrespectfully, a wife that spent too much money, a derogatory comment, a pick up line. The effect of any violation large or small is the same. It breaks our trust and wounds our spirit. We all know rejection at some point, we know betrayal, we know fear, and we know grief.

Every human being wrestles with fear, shame, loss or suffering at some point in their lives. Hope lies in the collective sound of our voices, our experiences and the living out of our lives. We are part of eternity and cannot escape it regardless of our belief systems.

Somebody else gets a kick out of debating science, politics, religion, world events, finance, the economy and the security of our people. Let them do it. I follow my heart, its message has not changed. If my story has value to anyone I hope it is to those who find themselves in unhealthy relationships. Those who have suffered abuse in all of its ugly forms. If you are in an unhealthy relationship, get out of it. If you have suffered abuse in your childhood tell someone about it.

My hope is that my story has value to those who have suffered loss and grief, illness and betrayal. Do not ignore it when anyone violates you. Also do not allow grief, guilt, shame or anger to defeat you. If you have wrong thinking; find out how other people think. If you have a problem, confront it. If you need help, ask for help.

If you are positioned in any of the systems, you know the problems. Talk about them. Foster partnerships and cooperation. Seek understanding and educate victims. We must stop allowing kids to fall through the cracks. Even though some systems failed me, many individuals did not. We can do better. I dropped the ball more than anyone else because I held it the longest. We need to become accountable together.

I hope my story has value to the normal people. If you find yourself to be one of those, share. Many will ask you to share your money. I will ask you to share yourself. Share your knowledge and your experience. Share your story. Use what you have to mentor a youth. Defend the cause of the poor and weak. If you have strength, courage, knowledge or talent share it with your loved ones and the people you meet on the street. The ones in your basement with your children, the ones in your backyard, your co-workers and your companions. It is the essence of you and your life, whichever part that sparks your passion that is the great gift to the living world.

The victory is our love for each other.

We are special treasures to the world if we allow ourselves to be. The battle is won by a simple strategy. Overcome evil with good. Learning to love myself has been my greatest challenge but I am learning to accomplish it. Writing my story nearly tore the heart, mind and guts right out of me.

I can tell you I struggled with writing it, especially the icky bits; I could not see any purpose or value in writing about it. I could only hope that purpose and value would be found. Even if only by just one person. And then I realized this story's purpose and value are living. Living things grow. I found both in writing it. I am the one person.

Despite almost going crazy while doing it, I had to submit to that little voice in my heart that said, *write it. Finish the story.* Thinking about it makes me laugh, remembering my own raging at God. I started writing the story first which led to asking about personal responsibility, which led to the rest.. I hope my story has value and purpose so I submit this to my own heart first, in which lives the spirit of love; and I submit it to you who read it, trusting my God to increase both.

Be well.

RESOURCES

www.isurvive.org

Printed in the United States
By Bookmasters